THE FLEECING
OF CHRISTIANITY

THE FLEECING OF CHRISTIANITY

TELEVANGELISM IN BIBLE PROPHECY

JACKIE ALNOR
FOREWORD BY AL DAGER

HighWay
A division of Anomalos Publishing House
Crane

HighWay
A division of Anomalos Publishing House, Crane 65633
© 2009 by Jackie Alnor
All rights reserved. Published 2009
Printed in the United States of America

09   1

ISBN-10: 0982211945 (paper)
EAN-13: 9780982211946 (paper)

A CIP catalog record for this book is available from the Library of
Congress.

Cover illustration and design by Steve Warner

All lowercase pronouns in reference to a deity are intentionally
used when an unbiblical god is referenced.

For Kristie

CONTENTS

FOREWORD

With all the exposition of scripture heard in the institutions we call "churches" today, there is scant attention paid by many to certain verses that are imperative to believers in Jesus in order to protect them from spiritual deception.

> Beloved, do not believe every spirit, but test the spirits whether they are of God, because many false prophets have gone out into the world. (1 John 4:1)

Even from among the early believers to whom the apostles ministered, there came out false prophets—false teachers—who were leading the unsuspecting and gullible away from the purity of the true Gospel. The enemy of our souls is clever; he knows how to couch his lies in terms that seem spiritually in tune with truth:

> For such are false apostles, deceitful workers, transforming themselves into the apostles of Christ. And no marvel, for Satan himself is transformed into an angel of light. Therefore it is no great thing if his ministers also be transformed as the ministers of righteousness, whose end shall be according to their works. (2 Cor. 11:13--15)

Through the centuries Satan has learned to adapt to the times and to the customs of the churches. Masquerading as ministers of righteousness, his ministers have learned the language of the faith. They have learned to say, "Jesus is Lord," in order to gain the confidence of God's saints and lead them on paths of unrighteousness, not so much in the flesh, but in the spirit.

At one time no unbeliever would confess that Jesus is Lord. So it was natural for the apostle Paul to write:

> Therefore I make known to you that no one speaking by the Spirit of God calls Jesus accursed, and no one can say that Jesus is Lord except by the Holy Spirit. (1 Cor. 12:3)

This was true at the time it was written because only true believers knew Jesus as Lord and would call Him "Lord." But since that time many false prophets have proclaimed, "Jesus is Lord," as a means to deceive the brethren into believing their lies.

The same misuse of truth may be said of John's statement:

> By this you know the Spirit of God: Every spirit that confesses that Jesus Christ has come in the flesh is of God, and every spirit that does not confess that Jesus Christ has come in the flesh is not of God. And this is the spirit of the Antichrist, which you have heard was coming, and is now already in the world. (1 John 4:2–3)

Today false religious cults and individual false teachers proclaim these truths that Jesus is Lord and that Jesus Christ has come in the flesh. As a result, many unsuspecting people, including brethren in Christ, have believed that these deceivers are of God.

So how are we to know the truth from the lie? How are we to test all things?

The only sure way to know the lie is to know the truth of God's Word—to study it diligently in order to show ourselves as approved workmen who need not be ashamed, rightly dividing the Word of Truth (2 Tim. 2:15).

Unfortunately, most Christians do not take the time or effort to do this. It is so much easier to sit in a pew and absorb what a trusted "pastor" tells them. If the proof texts he uses seem to fit, then what need is there to study further?

Easier still is to sit at home and watch television preachers expound their particular religious philosophy. Just as the world believes that, "if it's in the newspaper it must be true," so Christians believe that "if it's on Christian television," or "if it's on Christian radio," or "if it's in a Christian magazine," it must be true.

Well, it's time to chuck off the Pollyanna belief system engendered by the Christian media and face the reality that Satan is the prince of the power of the air (Eph. 2:2). He has proven himself quite adept at commandeering man's technology and manipulating the minds of those who avail themselves of it.

The airwaves are replete with satanic deceptions masquerading as God's light. It isn't that all those espousing these lies are conscientious agents of the satanic conspiracy; they are often among the deluded themselves—victims of Satan's schemes no less than those to whom they minister as ministers of righteousness.

Just because they appear saintly or knowledgeable of scripture doesn't mean they are ministers of righteousness. Just because they say, "Praise the Lord!" doesn't mean they even know the Lord Jesus.

In many cases they call the lord they praise "Jesus," but their lord's real identity is "Mammon"—wealth and power. They build their own not-so-little empires on the purses of the gullible and unknowledgeable. And it follows that as they distort scripture to gain filthy lucre, their doctrines more and more resemble the doctrines of demons. Spewing out various winds of doctrine that mislead honest, saintly people who have been remiss in diligently studying God's Word, they leave a wake of broken souls in their paths.

Yes, they cry; they swoon at the name of "Jeeeesuuuuuss"; they kiss babies in Africa while the cameras roll; they point to all the good works they do. But at the same time they are mesmerizing their viewers with their visual images of piety they distort God's Word and lead those viewers into ineffective lives of spiritual mediocrity.

Yet in the midst of all this loud confusion that seems so "holy," there have over the years been a few relatively unknown voices crying in the wilderness for people to repent of these sorceries and turn back to their first love in humility, and to develop a hunger for God's truth.

Just as Elijah heard God not in the wind, not in the earthquake, not in the fire, there are still, small voices calling out to the Body of Christ to turn back to God's truth and eschew the raging winds of Satan's doctrines masquerading as truth. These voices are striving to emulate Jude's admonition to the saints:

> Beloved, while I was very diligent to write to you concerning our common salvation, I found it necessary to write to you exhorting you to contend earnestly for the faith which was once for all delivered to the saints. For certain men have crept in unnoticed, who long ago were marked out for this condemnation, ungodly men, who turn the grace of our God into lewdness and deny the only Lord God and our Lord Jesus Christ. (Jude 1:3–4)

This book is one of those still, small voices. Jackie Alnor has been calling out to the saints of God for years, bringing a prophetic voice of correction against various deceptions that are plaguing the Body of Christ, and is helping readers see the spiritual errors in one particularly large deception.

Much of what is written in this book will no doubt fall on deaf ears (or eyes, in this case); much will be disregarded as "mean-spirited"—the voice of jealousy of an obscure writer among the many large, wealthy teachers to whom millions flock; much will be accounted as "unloving," "divisive," even "hateful."

This will be nothing new. Those who have been in this fight for so long have heard all the epithets of anger and disbelief from those who are comfortable in their deluded state. It is not to the naysayers Jackie writes as much as it is to the honest heart that seeks God's truth and is willing to learn the unpleasant realities of Satan's deceptions emanating from beloved public figures in the Christian media.

Yet I am certain that Jackie would agree with me as I challenge you, the reader, to test all things—even what is written herein—in order to come to knowledge of the truth. Find out if what is presented is true. What have you to lose but uncertainty about these things?

What have you to gain but the benefit of God's words of warning meant for the preservation of your soul?

May you grow in grace and in the knowledge of our Lord and Savior, Jesus Christ. To Him is the glory, both now and forever. Amen!

In Jesus' love,

Al Dager

Editor & Publisher of Media Spotlight

A Biblical Analysis of Religious & Secular Media

Redmond, WA

Acknowledgments

In Appreciation

First, I give praise and thanksgiving to my Lord and Savior, Jesus Christ, for the continual guidance and inspiration that kept me going throughout the work on this project and the shield of protection He provided.

Second, my sincere appreciation goes to Jacob Prasch and David Lister whose encouragement and support helped get me through many obstacles in the completion of the manuscript.

Third, to my sounding board, Janet Mayfield, for sharing my enthusiasm for the study of Bible prophecy and for helping me to flesh out what we were witnessing on Christian television and to put it in the big picture.

Fourth, a note of thanks goes out to many of my fellow discernment researchers who shared my burden for the victims of false teachers and shared their documentation with me to help expose error and take a stand for the Truth.

INTRODUCTION

Television has been a powerful force for the spread of the Gospel of Jesus Christ in the past fifty years. In the early days of television local stations would reserve their Sunday morning line-ups for Christian programming. It was seen as an obligation to the community. Shut-ins and others who could not make it to church could always count on finding an inspirational service in the comfort of their own living rooms.

The big three networks in the early days of television in America recognized that the airwaves were a public trust—the airwaves belonged to the people. Censor boards included clergymen who monitored programming to ensure that no unwholesome thing was broadcast that could corrupt the morals of the viewers.

All of that began to change in the 1960s and 1970s as the younger TV executives replaced the retirees. Archie Bunker upstaged Ward Cleaver. The Smothers Brothers trumped Lawrence Welk. Phil Donahue replaced Art Linkletter. What came first, the chicken or the egg? Did television change society or did society change television?

Today's popular programs include *Sex and the City, Desperate Housewives,* and *Will & Grace.* Children are watching *South Park* instead of *Sesame Street.* The quality of television programs has degraded to an all-time low.

The theme song to *Family Guy* sums it all up: "It seems today that all you see is violence in movies and sex on TV," Lois Griffin sings. "Where are those good old family values on which we used to rely?" adds her husband Peter. That is followed up with a half-hour of R-rated animated comedy.

As secular television has devolved, Christian programming has taken a similar course. Pat Boone and Anita Bryant are a distant memory. Today's Christian television networks broadcast an entire smorgasbord of teachers and entertainers. Good teaching is seen alongside bad teaching so that the truth gets muddled. Singers with surgically altered faces sing a variety of songs, some with biblical lyrics but mostly newer ones with deceptive messages.

Most Christian television networks try to compete with secular TV and are always way behind the times so that their worldly programming is always out-of-step with the fashion of the day. In trying to compete on the same level with the world, they become a laughingstock to the very ones they try to emulate. They are not taken seriously in their business.

The scandals over the years in televangelism are and continue to be an embarrassment to Bible-believing Christians. The greed and religious malpractice of "Christian" TV celebrities is a blight on church history. The selling of indulgences by Tetzel in Luther's day was petty theft compared to today's professional fleecers of the church of Jesus Christ who fleece the poor in order to get rich and do so tax-free.

CHRISTIAN PROGRAMMING

We cannot lump all Christian programs together and label them all odious. There are good shows and bad ones. One of the longest running programs is *The King is Coming*, hosted by Bible prophecy teacher Ed Hindson and seen on the Trinity Broadcasting Network (TBN). Howard Estep started the program in 1972 and after he passed away, Dave Breese hosted it from 1986 to 2002. All three men have taught the dispensational view of Bible prophecy and remained true to their biblical hermeneutic.

The Way of the Master is another excellent evangelistic program carried by many Christian television networks. It is hosted by Ray Comfort and former child star Kirk Cameron. They present a clear Gospel message in their man-on-the-street evangelism format.

But the bad religious programs far outnumber the good. There are some successful programs that are so pernicious that most Christian networks won't even carry them. They can be seen on networks such as the Black Entertainment Network (BET) and other lesser cable venues. They feature con men such as Leroy Jenkins, Don Stewart, Bishop Bernard Jordan, Robert Tilton, and Peter Popoff.

There are several major Christian TV networks that have grown larger with the new technologies of satellite and cable. Sky Angel carries fifty digital faith-based TV and radio channels. It started out as a satellite network that subscribers could access on their small satellite dishes. Now it is available by connection to the Internet and anyone with high-speed Web access can be a subscriber. Some of the television channels it carries are Faith TV, Cornerstone Television, the Inspiration Network, EWTN, and GodTV.

EWTN is the Catholic network that was founded by Mother Angelica, a spunky old nun peddling relics and rosaries. Some of its programming, such as *The Journey Home*, features Catholics who left Evangelicalism. Their guests testify of the supremacy of papal authority and how they rejected biblical Christianity for Rome.

Viewers of Sky Angel are treated to a variety of Christian programs that contradict one another. They can listen to radio programs that have solid Bible teachers, turn to GodTV to see founders Rory and Wendy Alec promote lying signs and wonders, and then turn to EWTN to hear Scott Hahn slam Christian fundamentalism.

TBN, the oldest and largest Christian TV network, was founded in 1973 by Paul and Jan Crouch, a silver-haired gentleman with his wife decked out in several pairs of false eyelashes and an assortment of bouffant wigs in shades of pink and purple. TBN has twenty thousand stations and is carried on many satellites. TBN has other networks within their network, including the Church Channel, JCTV Youth Network, and TBN Nejat, the Farsi network. TBN also produces films and has its own amusement park in Orlando, Florida called the Holy Land Experience.

TBN has led the way for the other Christian networks in their fundraising methods and their strategies for growth. Independently produced programs that buy airtime on TBN are also seen on the other networks. Faith teachers such as Fred Price, Kenneth Copeland, Benny Hinn, Marilyn Hickey, and Creflo Dollar cross-pollinate between networks. They can be seen virtually anywhere on the planet.

THE PROPHETIC BIG PICTURE

The Fleecing of Christianity will focus mostly on TBN since it is the leader in the field and shares its programs with the other networks. Christians need discernment now more than ever when watching religious programming. The mixture of true and false has created a mutant faith that Bible-believing Christians need to recognize and renounce. When Bible-believing Christians understand how the rise of wolves in sheep's clothing fits into Bible prophecy, their faith will be increased rather than shaken.

Does the rise of religious charlatans actually confirm the truth of the Bible? Are they a fulfillment of Bible prophecy? Is the prince

of the power of the air the real master of the airwaves? Could something started with good intentions be utilized for evil? Could Christian television play a key role in the events of the final hours of
history as we know it?

This book will attempt to unravel the mystery of iniquity that is
at work behind the scenes of history and will take a glimpse into the
ongoing hijacking of Christianity.

CHAPTER ONE

TRAILBLAZING TELEVANGELISTS

Oral Roberts and Kathryn Kuhlman are the Dynamic Duo of early Christian television. They laid the foundation in the 1960s that many others followed a decade later. There were other religious broadcasters in those days, such as Rex Humbard and Bishop Fulton Sheen, but Roberts and Kuhlman's influence is still seen today on all the major Christian networks.

Unfortunately, their code of ethics was based upon the love of the world, the lust of the flesh, and the foolish pride of life. Harsh words. But this chapter will document the sad legacy of these and other church leaders who were successful by the world's standards. But under the light of the Word of God, they are weighed and found wanting.

Perhaps not many Christians would fare much better with the amount of temptation thrown at those two. To whom much is given, much is required. Their success was their greatest impediment to overcoming sin. They had so much to protect and so much to lose if it all came crashing down. The devil, no doubt, honed in on them with his entire arsenal, aiming for the chink in their spiritual armor.

Jesus told His disciples, "For whoever desires to save his life will lose it, but whoever loses his life for My sake will find it" (Matthew 16:25).

The Bible records the downfall of many leaders in both the Old and the New Testaments. They are given for our instruction. We can learn from the mistakes of others and the victories too. Church history is the same. We can look back at the movers and shakers and see God moving in many situations that set the stage for a work He was doing. Some vessels were used for honor and some for dishonor and some for both. Martin Luther was chosen by God to restore the doctrine of grace to a church that had morphed into a legalistic, paganized system of works-righteousness. His nailing of the Ninety-five Theses on the door of that cathedral launched a movement that changed history. Yet at the end of his life he targeted the Jews for persecution and ended badly.

We are examining the development of Christian television, not to point blame to feel better about ourselves, but to make a course correction and exhort religious broadcasters to forsake the glitter of the world and get back on track. In these days of apostasy, that may look like a total waste of time, but if we can win even a few, it will be worth the effort.

SELF ON THE THRONE

The idea that man can become a god has its origin in the Garden of Eden. The devil used it to tempt Eve to rebel against God and eat the forbidden fruit.

"Then the serpent said to the woman, 'You will not surely die. For God knows that in that day you eat of it your eyes will be opened, and you will be like God, knowing good and evil'" (Gen. 3:4–5).

This lie of the devil is a foundational false teaching of the cult of

Mormonism, the Church of Jesus Christ of Latter Day Saints. Surprisingly, the Catechism of the Roman Catholic Church states, "For the Son of God became man so that we might become God."[1]

But how did this lie of the devil creep into the Evangelical church? It came by way of the Word/Faith movement from such luminaries as Kenneth Hagin, Kenneth Copeland, Frederick Price, and Charles Capps. It developed slowly, one error building upon an earlier error.

Popular televangelist T. L. Osborn wrote in his book, *You are God's Best*, "See yourself in God's image. Realize that you were never created to be poor, unhappy, dominated, manipulated, abused, shamed or walked on. You are created in God's class of being."[2]

Bishop Anne Gimenez, pastor of Rock Church in Virginia Beach, Virginia told her Daystar viewers, "I'm a new creation. You are a child of God. That means, listen to me, you are of God's species. Come on! You are of God-fabric."[3]

It is not much of a leap to go from being in God's class to being an actual god. As a god with a small *g* you call all the shots in your life. A new believer might begin his/her new life in Christ by submitting all things to the will of God, and then slowly begin to take back territory. What the new believer doesn't realize is that he/she has entered the spiritual battlefield on the first day he/she accepted Christ as Savior and Lord. A target is now on his/her back. The enemy begins the inner dialogue:

> Hey, you're a child of God and He has given you all things to enjoy. Don't worry about sinning—everyone sins. You're covered in the blood so it's okay to indulge yourself. After all, you've already lusted after him/her, so what's the difference if you carry it out? Nobody's perfect. You're a child of

the King—the wealth of the wicked is yours for the taking. You found that envelope with $100 in it. No need to look for the owner, God put it there for you...

The taking back of territory that should belong to God puts the person on his/her own throne and kicks God off it. At the core of the Word/Faith movement is the teaching that believers can create their own reality by the words of their confession. The titles of books written by the late Kenneth Hagin, the father of the faith movement, also known as the positive confession movement, conceptualize this error. They include *You Can Have What You Say, Write Your Own Ticket With God, Words, The Believer's Authority, The Midas Touch, Have Faith in Your Faith,* and many others. Justification for self-indulgence—even if scripture is used—is at the core of the faith movement. After all, the devil is the architect of scripture-twisting.

The late Evelyn Roberts, Oral's wife, demonstrated how the rationalization to shun God's will is arrived at. The words Jesus gave us as a model for prayer—"Thy will be done on earth as it is in heaven"—flies out the window:

> When Oral was on the bed with tuberculosis, [she told the TV audience] the ministers would come in and pray and one would say, "Lord, if it's your will, heal this boy." And the other would say, "Oh God, we know you put this on Oral so you could teach him a lesson." And then another would come along and say, "O God, save Oral so he won't go to hell." Well, you know, Oral didn't know if he wanted to go to heaven or not if that's the kind of God that was up there. If God didn't want to heal you, why would he want to save you? Why would you want to go where that kind of a god is?...Anytime people hear that God is a good God, that

Jesus wants them to be saved and healed…they will accept Him because He is a good God.[4]

Evelyn's former daughter-in-law, Patti Roberts [Thompson], wrote in her astonishing expose´ of her life in the Roberts family, *Ashes to Gold*, "The purification process has already begun. Much of what we attribute to Satan today is, I believe, the merciful judgment of God, the discipline of a loving Father."[5] So even a "good God" chastises His children. It's only spoiled brats who refuse correction.

Others in the Faith camp caught this rebellious spirit to substitute God's will for their own and to ridicule those who did not go along.

B.D. Hyman, daughter of movie star Bette Davis, hosting her own program on *Sky Angel* emulated Evelyn in a similar way. "Jesus tells us to have faith in God. Now what does that mean? It means the God kind of faith. The same kind of faith when God spoke and the world was formed…You can't go to God and say, 'Lord, if it be your will please heal me.' That's a silly prayer."[6]

A conversation between Kenneth Copeland and Pat Robertson on his *700 Club* broadcast demonstrates how widespread this is among Word/Faith teachers who dominate the airwaves. "A favorite prayer of unbelief of most people is 'O Lord, if it be thy will,'" Copeland said in a sing-song tone. "That's a faith killer from way back," Robertson chuckled.[7]

It wasn't much of a leap to go from having faith in your own will to becoming the god of your own universe. Paul Crouch, president of TBN back in the 1980s, became weary of defending his Faith friends such as Copeland and Earl Paulk, and in frustration shook his fist in the camera at those trying to bring correction and shouted, "I am a little god! Critics be gone!"[8]

Spiritual pride is at the core of the "we are little gods" teaching.

That concept fed into the idea that we are the masters of our own universe since it belongs to us as children of God. A common chant heard over and over again on Christian television by the Faith camp is, "We call the things that are not as though they are," something only God can do. Another word for this false belief is Positive Confession or euphemistically, "Blab-it-and-Grab-it."

It says that since God spoke the worlds into existence, we can use the same power of the tongue to create our own existence. Steve Munsey taught the Sky Angel viewers to put this divination into practice this way:

> I'm gonna train you through the word of God, teach you that you need to practice every day of your life calling those things which be not as though they were. You may be poor today, but stop saying you're poor. You are where you are today because you spoke it into existence in the past...You are going to declare that you are going to say those things that are not. I'm gonna start speaking like they are...What you speak is what you get. The Bible says life and death is in your tongues...Speak your future into existence![9]

Oral Roberts' son, Richard, led his TV audience in a chant while making a motion with his hands grabbing the air: "The Bible says the violent take it by force. Everybody just say, it's mine! Healing is mine in the name of Jesus."[10]

SEED-FAITH

This spiritual uprising began in the Faith camp with what is known as the Seed-Faith doctrine. Oral Roberts popularized the concept that money can be looked at as a seed you can sow, expecting a harvest of more money in return. It is a twisting of the Lord's parable of the sowing of the seed in the eighth chapter of Luke. Verse 11 identifies the seed as "the word of God."

Oral Roberts took a flying leap from that to seeing money as a seed from which a harvest of more money would grow if planted with that expectancy.

In his 1970 book, *Miracle of Seed-Faith*, Roberts explains the principle to his partners who would pledge money to him in what he called a "blessing-pact covenant." He wrote, "What I like about the blessing-pact covenant with God is that it is rooted in God, in seed that you plant unto Him, and in the solid feeling you gain in the inner man, knowing that He is going to give a miracle…But the blessing-pact works when, with simple, sincere faith in God, you work it."[11]

So Seed-Faith is a spiritual law, according to Roberts, that one could work at to get more money. He twisted the word of God to come up with the idea. He rewrote the verse that says, "It is more *blessed* to give than to receive," to say, "It is more PRODUCTIVE to give than to receive, for what we receive is not multiplied, but only what we give" (emphasis in original).[12] He explained, "SEED-FAITH is giving that you may receive. In doing this you give BEFORE you have received, not after."[13]

Seed-Faith is the mainstay upon which today's Christian television stations were built. Jesus warned us that we "cannot serve both God and Mammon," yet Christian television networks' very foundation is that lie of Satan: the worship of money.[14]

This was confirmed on a recent TBN *Behind-the-Scenes* broadcast when Paul Crouch Sr. and Paul Crouch Jr. interviewed their special guest Oral Roberts.

"As I flip through all of the other Christian stations," Crouch Sr. said, "everybody uses that tremendous Seed-Faith principle that the Lord gave you, how many years ago?"

"Sixty-one," said Roberts.

"Oh, only when we get to heaven will we know the wonderful worth," added Crouch.

"I think we know a lot now," replied the ninety-year-old faith healer, "because in virtually every full-gospel church in the world the pastor gets up and says, 'Now it's time to spread our seed,' and that was not a fact. And I know that you use it."

"Ohhhh, you bet we do. And it works!" Crouch Sr. beamed.

"Once or twice," added Crouch Jr. with a snicker.[15]

Jesus rebuked the Church of the Laodiceans in the book of Revelation for just this attitude: "You say, 'I am rich, have become wealthy, and have need of nothing'—and do not know that you are wretched, miserable, poor, blind, and naked" (Rev. 3:17).

The worst part of this scam is that it targets those who are the neediest—the sick and the poor. Roberts looked back to the time when he used to hold healing crusades in his giant tent in his 1971 autobiography, *The Call*. He wrote:

> Because our crusade attracted a large number of the unchurched and the sick, the offerings were many times below the budget of expenses. Churchgoing people are simply much more accustomed to giving. Then, too, many of the sick were in desperate financial straits because of heavy medical expenses.[16]

So since the poor and the sick found it too hard to give up what little they had, Roberts gave them the Seed-Faith spiel that promised them riches in return for giving till it hurt.

Today, the Seed-Faith idea has become a monster that is all over the television with an unlimited number of potential victims who buy into this idea of a spiritual lottery. (*More on this in Chapter 7: Spiritual Extortion.*)

One of the lowest perpetrators of Seed-Faith is TV con man Mike Murdock, seen regularly on the Inspiration Network carried on Sky Angel. Murdock apparently has no message other than money—he's a one-tune fiddle. I'd be afraid to buy a used car from this guy.

During a recent televised church service, he went into his disgraceful act while the pastor and Inspiration Network president David Cerullo sat on the platform looking on in full agreement.

Murdock badgered the congregation and the TV viewers to dig deep into their pockets. Merely tithing to the church wasn't good enough. "Tithing does not create prosperity. Tithing with expectancy creates prosperity…There ain't a woman in the world better looking than a hundred dollar bill…Don't you love more people when you got money?" Then he broke out in ridicule and said mockingly, "'I don't believe in giving so I can get something back.' How dumb thou art, how dumb thou art. If you rope your seed of expectation, God has no authorization to multiply it."[17]

It takes a real twisted person to mock the classic hymn "How Great Thou Art" like that. That is a horrible example of the worship of money and testing God's patience. What a surprise that the ground didn't open up and swallow him!

Roberts' Seed-Faith is also a regular fund-raising gimmick on the Daystar Television Network. On Daystar's program *Celebration*, guest Ellen Parsley, mother of televangelist Rod Parsley, put on a shameful performance utilizing the give-to-get mentality. She repeated over and over again that "poverty is a sin because God told you to multiply."[18]

Parsley brought a man up out of the audience who upon her

request took out his wallet and handed her a fist-full of dollar bills for her to do a demonstration. She took the money from him, laid it on the floor, and wallowed in it on the floor. When she was done, she shouted to him, "When I give it back you're going out in the holy ghost. Aaaaaah a hundredfold!" she screamed as she slipped the money back into the man's trousers. He did not "go out" (meaning being "slain in the spirit," a way televangelists knock people to the floor with their "power"), but remained standing with a grin on his face.

Parsley's distorted message was that God would not answer anyone's prayer without a bribe. "You can cry and scream and wail all you want to," she exhorted, "but until you're willing to come into covenant with God—God is a covenant God—until you're willing to lay some seed, some surety, some agreement upon your covenant and tell God what you want, you can just pray till your tongue falls out and you won't get the results that you really truly need. But the minute you come into covenant, lay surety upon the covenant and tell God what you want. You place a seed upon a need. You sow a seed upon a need. Why? Because that is a natural law and God does everything in the natural."

In one fell swoop Parsley just did away with miracles, which are defined as "a violation of the laws of nature."[19]

"Poverty is a curse," she continued ranting. "God wants you to be rich and very rich. I'm a child of the king! God don't want me walking around in rags. Oh rags, rags, rags! I'm a child of God! I ought to have diamonds on my fingers. I ought to wear the best clothes. Why? I'm a child of the King!"

As she railed on, the audience cheered her along.

In the Beatitudes, Jesus spelled out what our attitude toward giving and doing good to others should be. He said, "Give to everyone who asks of you. And from him who takes away your cloak, do not withhold your tunic either…And if you lend to those from whom you hope to receive back, what credit is that to you? For even sinners lend to sinners to receive as much back" (Luke 6:29b, 34).

Jesus also told us that "when you do a charitable deed, do not let your left hand know what your right hand is doing" (Matt. 6:3b).

We're told when we give not to do so under compulsion, but to give what we intend in our heart to give and to do that cheerfully, for God loves a cheerful giver. It is hard to imagine that anyone putting money in the offering after hearing Murdock or Parsley could do so cheerfully. This sort of coercion is a disgrace.

Patti Roberts has seen the fruit of this false teaching up close and in her book, *Ashes to Gold*, she shares the insights she received from the Lord into the deception she was once party to.

"The Seed-Faith theology that Oral had developed bothered me a great deal because I saw that, when taken to its natural extremes, it reduced God to a sugar daddy. If you wanted His blessings and His love, you paid Him off. Over and over again we heard Oral say, 'Give out of your need.' I began to question the motivation that kind of giving implied. Were we giving to God out of our love and gratitude to Him or were we bartering with Him?"[20]

"Oral thought I was splitting theological hairs, but it seemed supremely important to me. If we give to God because we think by giving we have somehow placed Him in our debt and He is now required to come through for us and meet our needs, we have, I believe, perverted the heart of the Gospel. Our only motive for giving should be love. When we encouraged people to give in order to have their needs met or so that they would receive 'a hundredfold in return,' I believed we were appealing to their sense of greed or desperation, neither of which seemed admirable to me. It was a wonderful fund-raising tool, but I believe it gave people a very unbalanced view of a very important biblical principle."[21]

Patti Roberts made the connection between the principles of Seed-Faith and the selling of indulgences at the time of the Reformation.

"Luther was incensed by the Church's practice of selling indulgences—offering forgiveness of sin and a shorter period of time in purgatory in return for gifts to the church, I had a very difficult time distinguishing between the selling of indulgences and the concept of Seed-Faith inflated to the degree to which we had inflated it."[22]

As demonstrated, the flagrant disregard for truth in this moneymaking scheme is more inflated than even Oral Roberts probably ever thought. Yet he is proud of his influence in the church and with the networks. We really do need a new Reformation that will nail these charlatans to the wall and get them off the airwaves by withholding our donations. They are not true representatives of Christ and His Church and have abused their positions.

TRICKS OF THE TRADE

Oral Roberts is a survivor. At the time of this writing he is ninety years old and living out his years in retirement in California in the lap of luxury. One historian of the modern Pentecostal movement wrote of Roberts and his contemporary big tent faith healers: "William Branham was a broken man after little more than a year; Jack Coe was physically exhausted at the time of his death; A.A. Allen, an incredibly tough campaigner, tottered constantly on the brink of psychological collapse; the resilience of Oral Roberts became a legend among his peers."[23]

Roberts Liardon (whose mother named him after the faith healer) produced a video series called *God's Generals* in which he paid tribute to these early tent revivalists. The top three from the 1940s were A.A. Allen, William Branham, and Jack Coe. Another video documentary of their lives was called *The ABCs of God*, an acronym of the first letter of their last names.

Liardon, a disgraced pastor who had been caught in a homosexual liaison, reported that these healing evangelists were very competitive with each other and would exaggerate their healings to one-up each other. They would even compete over the size of their huge tents and boast in their advertisements of having the largest one. "Jack Coe bought a tent and he stretched his poles just a few more inches all around so I guess it would be a few more feet larger than Oral Roberts."[24] And he added, "Back in those days, I guess, these guys wanted to have little discussions over who had the biggest tent."

Allen was defrocked by the Assemblies of God after being arrested for drunk driving. He died of liver problems due to acute alcoholism, according to Liardon.

Coe met his untimely death at the age of thirty-eight, attributable to his over-indulgent lifestyle. Liardon said that both Oral Roberts and Faith teacher Kenneth Hagin told Coe that if he didn't change in three areas God would remove him from the scene. These included his disagreeableness and nasty temperament, his love of money, and his overeating: attributes that are the norm in much of today's "Christian" television.

Another "general," William Branham, also died young after denouncing the doctrine of the Trinity and joining Oneness Pentecostalism. He was a certified heretic who claimed he couldn't do any healing until his personal angel showed up—an unbiblical concept that is still taught in some circles today. Due to Branham's apparent signs and wonders, many modern-day "prophets" consider him to be the greatest prophet since John the Baptist. But their criteria are not biblical. According to the Gospel of John, John the Baptist did no miracles (John 10:41), yet Jesus acknowledged, "Among those that are born of women there is not a greater prophet than John the Baptist" (Luke 7:28).

A lesser-known healing tent revivalist in those days was a man by the name of O. L. Jaggers, who shared the stage with the others. He didn't die young but he went off his rocker, evident by his inability to teach from any book of the Bible except Revelation with his own demented interpretations of being at the center of it. In the 1980s he could be seen on local television in Los Angeles, dressed in a blinding gold robe, wearing an awkward hairnet, televising from his Universal World Church. He claimed to have the holy of holies behind a curtain on his stage. He also said he had the tree of life whose leaves you could eat to live forever. He died a broken and crazy man.

The healing evangelists copied one another's styles in several ways. They would wear white suits, have dramatic demonstrations of healing prayers, and use organ music to heighten the mood.

By the time the flamboyant Kathryn Kuhlman came on the scene, she had perfected these methods of creating the right atmosphere for "miracles." Although Kuhlman never met Aimee Semple-McPherson, the founding pastor of Angelus Temple and founder of the Foursquare Gospel denomination, she emulated her style. She even adapted Semple-McPherson's vocal intonations and physical mannerisms. Kuhlman's biographer, Jamie Buckingham described her stage presence in his 1976 book, *Daughter of Destiny.*

> Kathryn said she had nothing to do with the healings. In a sense that was true. She was only the catalyst which brought the power and the people together. Yet, in another sense, she had everything to do with the miracles, for she had put together a "workable package" through which the Holy Spirit was able to market His product: miracles.[25]

If her powers were truly of the Holy Spirit, she certainly wouldn't need to help God out by putting together some "workable package." In fact, according to Buckingham, she could not accomplish any miracles unless the audience kept their focus upon her. He wrote:

> The greatest secret was Kathryn herself. She insisted on being the focus. She never sat down during those four and five-hour meetings, even when Dino was playing…In fact, she was always doing just a little something to keep the audience's attention on herself. To the critical eye it seemed she was "upstaging"—raising her hand when Jimmie hit a high note…and making some grand gesture when Dino finished his playing. It seemed like the epitome of ego, always demanding the spotlight. But the more discerning ones saw it as wisdom. Kathryn knew about the necessity of spiritual focus. She would never allow anyone to take the microphone away from her. [26]

Buckingham also recalled Kuhlman's strategy of placing "men of the cloth" in visible locations towards the front of the platform. She felt that priests and nuns in full clerical regalia lent credibility to her ministry. He recalls the time that a Trappist monk was slain in the spirit at Kuhlman's touch and she added a flair of drama to it. He wrote:

> Kathryn didn't move. She stood, transfixed, one finger pointed heavenward, the other hand stretched out toward the silent man on the floor, her face uplifted. Glowing… Kathryn never touched him, never said a word. She just stood still, her finger pointing toward God, her face lifted, bathed in an unearthly light. The only sound was the gentle

music from the organ and the muted gasps from the audience each time the Roman Catholic monk sank to the floor under the slaying power of the Holy Spirit.

It was as though there was surrounding her an aura of power. Anyone inside that aura could hardly stand. I had the feeling that had Kathryn moved a muscle, she, too, would have gone down—so great was the power of God. The same aura often appeared around her while she was ministering. On occasions it caused her face to actually glow.[27]

The word "aura" is used a lot by people who were close to Kuhlman. Many testified of William Branham in the same way. In fact, there's a famous photograph of Branham with what appears to be an unearthly light like a halo over his head. Followers of the faith healers never stopped to ask themselves if these manifestations were of God or metaphysical antics of an angel of light. The faith healers had a lot of blind followers who loved the show and didn't think anything at all about the fact that Kuhlman dressed like a witch, wearing dresses that simulated a witch's outfit—only in white.

How strange that she would have power to "slay in the spirit" a Trappist monk, a Catholic priest who bows to a monstrance and claims to have the power to turn a wafer into the actual body, blood, soul, and divinity of Christ. (The Trappists are known for their contemplative prayer, a type of mindless meditation they borrowed from Zen Buddhism.)

Kuhlman's religious spirit had a close kinship with others of dubious orthodoxy. Buckingham wrote that Catholic clergymen who sat behind her on the platforms actually helped to "create the proper climate of trust and understanding which was so necessary for a miracle service."[28] It is hard to believe that Jamie Buckingham or any Protestant could say this with a straight face.

Benny Hinn, who claims Kuhlman's mantle, also warms up to Roman Catholics and identifies with their mysticism. He copies her use of loud repetitious music to set a mystical ambiance to prep the crowd to expect miracles. Buckingham noted that "the musical climate was inestimably important in creating an atmosphere in which the Holy Spirit could move with freedom and ease."[29]

This makes no sense whatsoever from a biblical standpoint. Jesus and the apostles certainly didn't have traveling musical accompaniment in order for the Holy Spirit to pour out spiritual gifts. Who played the gig at the upper room on the day of Pentecost? Yet today virtually all "Christian" rallies that advertise signs and wonders begin with loud driving music before any unearthly manifestations can drop down out of the other dimension.

That is not to say that the gifts of the Spirit are not for today. God has not forsaken His church. Jesus is still in our midst. But we must do things God's way, not man's way or the way of the occult. The Bible's instructions for the laying on of hands on the sick do not call for a circus atmosphere to hype people up to create a "miracle" that follows some sort of spiritual principle. James asks, "Is anyone among you sick? Let him call for the elders of the church, and let them pray over him, anointing him with oil in the name of the Lord. And the prayer of faith will save the sick, and the Lord will raise him up" (James 5:14–15a).

A pastor friend of mine keeps a vial of oil with him wherever he ministers and is quick to pray a prayer of faith for the sick. He does not need to refer the sick in his congregation over to the latest stadium event hoping for the stirring of the atmosphere.

Oral Roberts argues that the sick seeking healing need "a point of contact" to focus their faith upon in order to have a healing miracle. His point of contact was his right hand that would tingle when the "healing virtue" was present for healing. Kuhlman's point of contact was herself—people needed to stare transfixed at her for any results. And both of them told the viewers at home to place their hands on their television sets as a point of contact with the divine. I don't think they can give chapter and verse for that one!

Paul Crouch Jr. was anticipating Oral's answer to a nagging question he had when he and his father were interviewing Roberts. "Oh, I'm dying to ask this," the younger Crouch said. "You know we asked this of R. W. Schambach, but you know you've seen millions of miracles and healings—what's one of the greatest miracles that you've ever seen in your ministry to date?"[30]

Oral didn't skip a beat. "Little Willie Phelps of Lynchburg, Virginia," was his response. He went on to tell the story of an eleven year old who needed crutches to walk due to a short leg that forced him to wear a body brace. Roberts was leaving his crusade and was stopped by the boy who told him that he heard from God that he was going to be healed that day. Roberts hesitated, telling him he was tired and couldn't get up his anointing when he's tired, but said a quick faithless prayer over him anyway. Well, he saw Willie the following year, and lo and behold, he was running up to him without his brace.

"I looked at him; 'You're that little boy I prayed for a year ago,'" said Roberts. "He said, 'I am.' He said he went to school and almost broke up the class cause the boys had been mean to him…and his teacher had him get up to the front and tell the story and he said, 'Son, that must have cost lots of money,' and Willie Phelps said, 'Teacher, it didn't cost a dime.' That may have been one of the greatest miracles that I've ever had."

The father and son Crouches looked stunned and under-impressed. "Was he instantly healed in front of you or as he left?" asked Junior Crouch.

"I have no idea," answered Roberts in a moment of sheer honesty. "I just prayed...but I did not know if he were healed until a year later."

Wow, sixty-one years of ministry as a healing evangelist and that's the best one he could come up with. He didn't even do the leg-lengthening trick on the boy that other faith healers have so much fun doing. He just prayed for the child and the child recovered. He just did it the Bible way and the boy was healed. No flashing lights; no sounds of a trumpet. God just healed the boy!

A week later, flamboyant televangelist R. W. Schambach was a guest on TBN's *Praise the Lord* program while Dwight Thompson was guest hosting. Thompson asked Schambach the same question:

"Dr. Schambach, you could write volumes of books of things that you have seen in the ministry: healings and miracles. I know that you're in the process, if you haven't already completed it, a great book, and kind of a catalogue of some of the things you've seen. Just talk to us out of your heart of what you've seen."

"There's so many," Schambach responded. "In sixty years, I mean you can't even remember everything that God done [*sic*]. I've seen God grow legs on bodies. I've seen God put an eyeball back in a woman's socket that was taken out. This is something you know that is visible...God is a miracle-working God."[31]

What a contrast! Sounds like a heck of a lot of exaggeration—but then again Schambach got his start with A. A. Allen who was good at spinning a yarn.

Several years ago Schambach was on the TBN *Praise-a-thon* boasting that he "saw God put four fingers right back on a lady's hand."[32] "I don't know how God does this. It's a creative miracle." Of course, even though these meetings are all televised not one of these so-called "creative miracles" has ever been caught on tape.

Pentecostal historian David Harrell Jr., after years of research and attending these crusades, offered this insight: "Long sensitive to charges of fraud and deception because of his healing claims, Roberts had developed a complete philosophy of divine healing by the 1960s. He increasingly associated health with a positive mental attitude and the belief that 'God is a good God.' In an interview with Mike Douglas in 1970, Roberts agreed that much of the healing he effected had to do with psychosomatic illness, but he insisted that it was nonetheless valuable."[33]

Kuhlman's record wasn't much better than Roberts. One of her healing crusade physicians who interviewed patients claiming a healing was interviewed in *McCall's Magazine* in September 1994, in an article called, "In Search of a Miracle." He told *McCall's*, "In talking to these people, I tried to be as honest, understanding and objective as possible, but I couldn't dispense with my medical knowledge and my common sense. I listened carefully to everything they told me and followed up every lead that might have led to a confirmation of a miracle. I was led to an inescapable conclusion: Of the patients who had returned to Minneapolis to reaffirm the cures claimed at the miracle service, not one had, in fact, been miraculously cured of anything."[34]

Roberts never really had much of a relationship with Kathryn Kuhlman. Her biographer pointed to her insecurities for not wanting to keep company with what she saw as the competition. She used to secretly attend Roberts' meetings, hiding in the back of darkened auditoriums to size up the crowd. At one meeting she attended incognito, she turned to her friend and whispered, "We had a bigger crowd this afternoon, didn't we?" She reportedly would snipe at Roberts in the press or even in sermons. "When his ministry changed from healing to education and he opened his multi-million dollar university in Tulsa, Kathryn commented, 'He always was good at raising money.'"[35] Oral Roberts bestowed ORU's first of many honorary doctorates upon Miss Kuhlman in 1973.

Later in life whatever spirit was said to be upon Kuhlman left her. At one of her last meetings she reportedly tried desperately to conjure up some power, but nothing happened. When she couldn't knock anybody over, Buckingham felt sorry for her and fell over on purpose into the waiting arms of a catcher. He said he loved her too much to disappoint her.

LIVE LIKE ROYALTY

There are certain fringe benefits that accompany being a religious television star. But all of them can ensnare the unsuspecting soul.

TV stars have adoring fans. There are Christian celebrities and musicians who literally have groupies that follow them from place to place. Egos get inflated no matter what your theology happens to be.

Patti Roberts lived it and saw close-up how believing one's own publicity can distort one's self-concept. She wrote:

> The use of television as our primary means of ministry created a paradox and a problem for us. While television enabled us to reach more people, it also allowed us to remain very remote…Power corrupts…We seem to have a perverse tendency to want to create idols. Whether they are golden calves or Christian superstars…But no man or woman can stand the weight of worship. It is intoxicating and highly addictive. It perverts one's way of thinking and bends one's personality. The load is too much. You lose sight of who you are in God.[36]

Dru Axtell, former co-host of a TBN-sponsored program, *Marriage on the Rock*, that won an Angel Award, was startled the first time she detected worship directed towards her. In her excellent book, *I Thought it was God*, she wrote, "About that time, when we would walk down the aisle to go on the stage, sometimes people would reach out and touch us. That really alarmed me, and I'd get on stage and be sure to tell them, 'You have got to look to Jesus…You cannot base your faith on us.'…I heard myself cry out of my spirit, 'God, I feel like I have started a cult!'"[37]

These two women learned the hard way just how seductive stardom in the "Christian" television industry can be and what snares are in place to shipwreck one's faith. They got out with their spiritual lives intact. Others are not so fortunate—even if they still live in mansions and can make the claim, "I am rich and in need of nothing."

Axtell warns others who might be "drawn into television ministry, have your guard up against the glory getting to you. Remember, pride comes before the fall. Also, do not fall victim to the 'Messiah complex'—thinking you are so powerful and special the rules do not apply to you."[38]

Fame was certainly a snare for Kathryn Kuhlman. She became obsessed with keeping an eye on her own popularity. Buckingham reported, "She read every review, every article about her that appeared in all those Sunday newspaper magazines across the nation. It was as though she actually drew sustenance from them, even the bad ones. At least she was being recognized, and that human side of her seemed to need it to keep going."[39]

Kuhlman would rub elbows with Hollywood's stars and instruct her ushers to seek them out in the crowd and report back to her where they were sitting. She also had a private audience with Pope Paul VI at the Vatican. She had her photograph taken with him and made sure it got distributed via news releases to be seen by her adoring public. Bible-believing Christians were not impressed that she was blessed by the "vicar of Christ." But she was honored by his acknowledgment.

Another fringe benefit for both Kuhlman and Roberts was the wealth they amassed, allowing them to live like royalty. Kuhlman had expensive taste in clothing and jewelry and she was a collector of antique furniture. She only stayed at the best luxury hotels and shopped in Beverly Hills at I. Magnin's. It was reported that after she died she had over seventy-five expensive pulpit dresses stored in her basement in addition to closets full of fancy threads.

The Roberts family also indulged in conspicuous consumption. Patti Roberts devotes much space in her tell-all book to the spare-no-expense attitudes of the Roberts dynasty. She had to come to grips with her own lust for material goods. She wrote of her transformation from an ordinary life to an extravagant one after marrying Richard Roberts:

> We went from living in a duplex and driving one old American car to owning an expensive home and driving foreign luxury cars; from buying local, ready-made, off-the-rack clothing to ordering the finest Italian suits, silk ties and hand-crafted leather accessories. We justified our increasingly lavish life styles because all of our efforts were directed toward building a Christian empire...I rationalized that I was the wife of the head of a major corporation and therefore we could live like the heads of other major corporations. Between tapings for the TV show, we often took expensive and lengthy vacations and soon established a sort of "jet set life style."[40]

When she finally wised up she had a face-to-face confrontation with a gold swan that was the bathtub faucet. Her repentance for being a part of using underhanded means to market the church was the downfall of her marriage. After her divorce, Richard Roberts found a more suitable wife, Lindsay, whose conscience didn't appear to trouble her when she would use ministry money to decorate her mansion or go on five-star vacations. (Richard and Lindsay were recently embroiled in a scandal at Oral Roberts University where Richard Roberts was forced out as president for financial misman-agement. ORU professors accused the Roberts of using ORU funds for fancy vacations and accused Lindsay of spending money on young male coeds with whom she would frequently exchange text messages.)

Oral Roberts started out determined not to misuse ministry funds, but that apparently changed over time. He wrote in his 1971 autobiography, "I reaffirmed that under no circumstances would I accept personal gifts from anyone whether they were large or small. Gifts sent to me personally would automatically be turned over to the Evangelistic Association for disbursement…I have often offended people because I refused the money they tried to put in my hand after I had prayed for them. I had promised God I would not touch the gold or the glory. I meant it."[41]

Today, Roberts sings a different tune. During his October 17, 2008 visit to TBN, he instructed people that if they wanted to give him any financial gifts, just make them payable to Oral Roberts with a personal note written on it and Tulsa would forward them to him in California.

Like the Roberts family, Kuhlman's expensive tastes were often seen as scandalous. Not long before she passed away, she ended her longtime association with pianist Dino Kartsonakis. Her biographer reported that her relationship with Dino sometimes appeared scan-dalous and that her staff referred to him as a "gigolo," despite the comparisons many made of Dino as a "Christian" Liberacé. After hiring him, she reportedly bought him an expensive wardrobe, even flying him to Italy to have his suits tailored. After several years of working together, Dino fell in love with a former showgirl named Debby Keener and that enraged Kuhlman who gave him an ultimatum. He chose his showgirl. (His current wife, Cheryl, is not the same girl.)

Dino's brother-in-law, Paul Bartholomew who was Kuhlman's personal administrator and handled the distribution of her television program, was also served notice.

Los Angeles Times reporter Russ Chandler reported that "Dino said he quit the ministry because of alleged inconsistencies he observed between her professional image and her personal life. 'Her double standard of living had paid its toll on my conscience,' he said."[42]

Bartholomew wrote a book about his experiences and observations of Kathryn Kuhlman's ministry that he carried around with him. In an out-of-court settlement between him and Kuhlman for monies he said were due him, he agreed to a ten-year moratorium on publishing anything about Kuhlman. However, the manuscript that Kuhlman desperately wanted to keep out of the public eye mysteriously disappeared out of Bartholomew's locked car. What goods he had on Kuhlman, if any, we may never know. But Bartholomew told this author that he could discern that Kuhlman's associates knew the secret contents of his manuscript by comments made to him that no one who had not read it could have known.

Kathryn Kuhlman died on February 20, 1976 at the City of Faith hospital after receiving prayer from Oral himself. The surgeons couldn't fix her abdominal obstruction. She was sixty-eight years old. She was buried at Forest Lawn Memorial Park in Glendale, California, the same cemetery as her role model, Aimee Semple-McPherson.

Oral Roberts and Kathryn Kuhlman were certainly trailblazers in the milieu of Christian media. Some might wonder why God would allow Christian television to flourish if it is following the standards of a world on the brink of judgment. Perhaps God allows it to test us to see if we will be faithful to him or chase after our idols. Judgment begins in the house of God and all of us are being tested before the world is judged. From a biblical worldview Roberts and Kuhlman failed the test. The champions are women like Patti Roberts Thompson and Dru Axdell.

Axdell and Thompson are the heroines of this sad story. They are the blessed ones. Axdell said it all when she wrote:

> The ministry was my bread and butter, but I preferred to tell the truth and go into secular work than to tickle their ears with what some wanted to hear to keep the money coming in. God help us! As I end this writing, I have gone through bankruptcy and divorce…Now I am working at Burger King…A real lesson in humility, maybe? It was quite a change from silk dresses on stage in Beverly Hills to bending over a hot broiler and steamer.[43]

"Better is a little with the fear of the Lord, than great treasure with trouble" (Proverbs 15:16).

CHAPTER TWO

THE END TIMES AT TBN

PROPHECY 101

Paul Crouch Sr., president and founder of the Trinity Broadcasting Network (TBN), believes that the Lord Jesus Christ is going to return to planet Earth to set up His prophesied one-thousand-year Kingdom.[44] Not all professing Christians believe in this doctrine of the millennial reign of Christ. Many spiritualize away clear passages of scripture to come to a different conclusion.

The earth will enjoy a thousand years of peace at that time. One famous reference to this time of peace is inscribed on the United Nations Headquarters building in New York City. It reads: "And they will beat their swords into plowshares, and their spears into pruning hooks," which is taken from Isaiah 2:4. This passage identifies this time period as "the Day of the Lord," and adds that "nation shall not lift up sword against nation, neither shall they learn war anymore." What a wonderful promise!

The prophet Isaiah prophesied this as a literal time on earth when all of nature will be in harmony and the Lord Himself will be ruling from His throne in Jerusalem. At that time people will again live to be hundreds of years old and will live side by side with the resurrected saints who are in their resurrected bodies.

But before the return of Christ, there will be a seven-year period of time in which the devil has his last stand in the person of the antichrist. This is known as the "Great Tribulation" or "the time of Jacob's Trouble." The Bible gives a lot of details about this time in the Book of Revelation and in the Book of Daniel as well as in the Gospels and Epistles.

Christians need to be aware of Bible prophecies regarding the last days as an inoculation against error at a time when spiritual deception will be at an all-time high.

There are many indicators that we are nearing the time of the end and the imminent return of our Lord. Jesus gave us a prophetic pattern to look for in the twenty-fourth chapter of Matthew's Gospel. These signs would come in waves like the birth pangs of a woman in labor, stronger and closer together. Here is a list of the beginning of sorrows:

- False christs, i.e., false anointings
- Wars and rumors of wars
- Famine
- Pestilence, i.e., by both disease-causing single-cell pests and insects
- Earthquakes in diverse places
- Proliferation of false prophets and religious deceivers

The coming Tribulation period is a time of God's judgment upon a Christ-rejecting world. Jesus likened the time to the days of Noah, which was a time when the wickedness of man was great in the earth. He also compared it to the time of Lot, Abraham's nephew, who lived in Sodom, the town God destroyed along with Gomorrah, when He rained down fire and brimstone.

In the case of Sodom and Gomorrah, God was able to isolate His judgment on the wicked to those two towns. But in the case of Noah, all the inhabited land was corrupt, so His judgment was universal—worldwide. After the flood, God promised He would never again destroy all flesh by water, but that the next global judgment would be one of fire:

> But the heavens and the earth which are now preserved by the same word, are reserved for fire until the day of judgment and perdition of ungodly men. (2 Pet. 3:7)

One need only look around to see that the whole earth is ripe for judgment. Evil is not isolated to one locale—it is universal. Therefore God's judgment will have to be universal because He cannot stamp out evil by destroying one city. But before He can execute judgment, He will rescue those who have the righteousness of Christ by faith, since it is not His will to destroy the good along with the evil.[45]

When the cup of iniquity of the wrath of God is full, then it will be outpoured. Futurists look at nuclear proliferation to determine the time on the Armageddon clock that usually is seen as a few minutes before midnight. But a better signifier of the nearness of the coming judgment is the increase of evil in the world and the backsliding of the professing church.

Recognizing the signs of the times does not guarantee you'll escape the coming calamities. That depends entirely on your right standing with God. The prophet Amos warned:

> Woe to you who desire the day of the Lord! For what good is the day of the Lord to you? It will be darkness, and not light. (Amos 5:18)

Some self-righteous folks are going to be in for a rude awakening on that day. I am convinced that after the rapture occurs, the churches will still be full of people and TBN and other "Christian" networks will not go black.

TBN IN BIBLE PROPHECY?

Those in TBN's inner circle are bold to see themselves in Bible prophecy in dramatic ways. TBN has over twenty thousand stations, cable networks, the Internet, and is carried on seventy satellites[46] that beam its programming around the world. The senior Crouch interprets the angel mentioned in Revelation 14:6 that flies through the midst of heaven as these satellites, even though they also happen to carry X-rated programming as well.

"You know I've told you this little story so many times, but I have found a scripture in the Bible that talks about satellites," Crouch asserted during one of their fund-raisers they call Praise-a-thon. "I promise you! Listen to this! Isaiah 45:8: 'Drop down ye heavens from above. Let the skies pour down righteousness. Let the earth open. Let them bring forth salvation. I, the Lord have created it.' That's satellite, brother! Pure and simple! The heavens are opening and the skies are pouring down righteousness."[47]

"I heard Billy Graham say that," Crouch added. "Billy Graham fully believes that Revelation 14:7—'I saw another angel flying through mid heaven'—Those satellites fly in mid-heaven, not the lower heaven, not the far-out heaven, but that's exactly where they fly—mid-heaven. One—with the everlasting Gospel, preaching to them that dwell upon the earth, saying with a loud voice, 'repent for the hour of his judgment has come.'"[48]

Crouch has been promoting this ever since TBN got its first satellite link-up. Since the angel in Revelation is in the singular, it was almost tenable. After all, if the demon locusts in the ninth chapter of the book of Revelation are actually helicopters, as some interpret, then you could take it a step further and interpret the angel to be a satellite. But seventy satellites? That's a lot harder to fit into the passage.

Crouch interprets another verse as referring to satellites in Revelation 1:7—"And every eye shall see Him—via satellite"—a headline stated in the March 1990 TBN newsletter. So according to Crouch, TBN is the vehicle by which God gathers the final harvest. Therefore, Jesus cannot return until TBN fulfills the Great Commission of sending the Gospel out around the world.

"I believe John saw a satellite," Jan Crouch joyfully proclaimed. "I've heard Billy Graham and Chuck Smith and everybody say that. I mean what else would that be? All of heaven opens up and he saw what he recorded in the book of Revelation for us and all of a sudden he saw us. He saw us in his vision laying there when the world thought he was all alone...and there he was having this vision of us carrying the good news via satellite around the whole wide world... Is that awesome?"[49]

Even before TBN got onto a satellite, Crouch read TBN into Bible prophecy. Quoting Acts 2:19, in the July, 1986 TBN newsletter: "And I will show wonders in heaven above, and signs in the earth beneath." Crouch wrote, "The FCC had GRANTED EIGHT TV station permits in ONE DAY! This has broken all records at the FCC...Surely this must be a part of the SIGNS AND WONDERS IN HEAVEN spoken of by the Prophet Joel" (emphasis in original).

TBN ENCODED IN THE BIBLE

TBN's importance has been attested to by many of the Crouches' friends and TBN regulars. And in every case Paul and Jan Crouch give hearty approval to the visions and revelations that elevate TBN above the competition.

One claim is that Paul, Jan, and TBN are God's appointed Noah's Ark for the last days. According to a guest on the *Praise the Lord* program that aired in early January, 2001, their names are supposedly encrypted in the book of Genesis in the passage where Noah loaded the survivors of the flood into the ark.

This revelation was made possible by the Bible code theory, an unorthodox means of interpreting the Bible. This method of soothsaying was made popular by the book *The Bible Code*, written by non-Christian author Michael Drosnin. This book has now become a fad in fringe Bible prophecy teaching circles. However, no reputable Bible scholar acknowledges it as a valid way of studying scripture.

Co-hosting the program that evening was Ben Kinchlow, former *700 Club* co-host, who told the audience that this latest discovery was proof that God's word is of supernatural origin. Their guest that night was Paul Crouch's personal Bible code decoder, Yacov Rambsel, whom Crouch commissioned to write a book that was a love gift for TBN donors. The book is called, *The Genesis Factor*. "I honestly believe God is revealing it to us in these last days," said Crouch, "to unseal this book (holds up the Bible) and tell us things that no other generation has ever known."

According to Rambsel, the clue to how the words in the Bible are to be understood is revealed in the book of Daniel. "In Daniel, where it says at the time of the end knowledge shall be increased," explained Crouch, "encoded in that passage right there are the words 'Bible codes.'"

Rambsel uses what he calls equidistant letter sequences (ELS) to find hidden messages in the Hebrew words of scripture. [It's reminiscent of the backward masking craze, seeking hidden messages on rock albums by playing the albums backwards.] Various critics have shown that virtually any message can be extracted from the Bible through this method.

Rambsel explains in his book how he found the ministry of TBN encrypted in Genesis 7:13, where Noah is gathering his family and all the animals into the ark. "It's the ark of refuge," said Rambsel, "He's talking about salvation."

"So what we find in that little passage," said Crouch, reading from *The Genesis Factor,* "is as they're loading everybody on the ark, starting with the third letter in the eighth word and counting forward every fifteenth letter, spells 'Paul'…adjacent to his name at the same ELS is 'Jan,' which is the name of his wife…starting with the fourth letter in the third word, counting every twentieth letter spells 'TBN.' Adjacent letters in the same ELS spell at least eleven different words that are directly associated with the work of TBN: Paul; Jan; last name Crouch; good news; satellite; film; praise; shall be clothed with faith; information and knowledge. It's all there!"

Crouch was quick to point out that his is not the only name encrypted in the Bible. "We honestly believe, Yacov, don't we, that everybody's name is encoded in the Holy Bible?"

"I know this for a fact," agreed Rambsel. "Absolutely!"

"So this is no special blessing to Jan and me," Crouch added. "We believe that's the Book of Life, but there's another book, the Lamb's Book of Life. That you have to be born again before you get into that book."

Perhaps the Crouches and their Bible decoder are picking up these ideas from their friends without realizing it. Back on December 5, 1999, on Benny Hinn's *This Is Your Day* telecast, faith healer Oral Roberts told Hinn that Hinn and his ministry were the ark.

"They, as a body, are coming together in climax," said Roberts, referring to Christians of all persuasions. "For example, your crusades is being borne up to the faith of the body of Christ [*sic*] and the pressing needs of humanity in the same way that the ark of Noah and his family was born up by the waters that will destroy the world. The great rain and flood that came also was lifting the ark. And when sin came to a climax, righteousness came to a climax in Noah just like it's coming to pass in your life, in your ministry."

The potential for evil from this Bible code trend is almost infinite. Can you imagine the Lord Jesus looking at scripture that way? No right-thinking believer in Christ would. With God there is "no variation or shadow of turning" (James 1:17). Jesus said, "I spoke openly to the world. I always taught in synagogues and in the temple...in secret I have said nothing" (John 18:20). God never gave man any such method of interpreting scripture.

TBN: THE SOURCE OF THE SPIRIT'S POWER

Country-gospel singer Betty Jean Robinson has been a TBN mainstay almost from the beginning. She has her own show on TBN called *Up On Melody Mountain*. She is most famous for her beautiful contemporary Christian song, "He is Jehovah." Inside her Bible, she keeps tucked away a handwritten account of a vision she received some twenty years ago. It reads: "I saw the whole map of America, and in the center was the presidential seal...But the eagle on the seal was looking toward TBN in Southern California. From TBN in Southern California great beams of light began to flood up over America and across the world! Written on those beams of light was: 'Salvation, Deliverance and Power,' and then a great beam that said, 'CANNOT BE STOPPED!' And then I heard the Spirit say to me, 'I have let my servant Paul in on the secrets for the final days.'"[50]

This vision allegedly occurred years before the opening of TBN's International Production Center (IPC) in Irving, Texas, which was designed after the White House and where their programming is translated into many languages. It is hard to say if this vision inspired the design of that studio or if the studio was a fulfillment of Betty Jean's vision, which is the TBN interpretation.

But the most lofty claim of TBN's value in the last days come from the Crouches' personal prophet, Benny Hinn. One night he made a statement that flabbergasted Paul and Jan, who listened with their heads bowed and their hands raised to heaven.

"Here's first what I see for TBN," Hinn began. "You're going to have people raised from the dead watching this network."[51]

"I'm telling you, I see this in the spirit," Hinn continued. "It's gonna be so awesome. Jesus, I give you praise for this—that people around the world, maybe not so much in America. People around the world who will lose loved ones will say to the undertakers, 'Ahh not yet. I want to take my dead loved one and place him in front of the TV set for 24 hours.'"

"Placing them before a television set, waiting for God's power to come through and touch them. It's gonna happen time and time, so much it's gonna spread [sic]."

Hinn's story kept growing as he spoke that night, testifying that he saw caskets lining up in front of TV sets that had TBN tuned in. He said that loved ones would place the cadavers' hands on the TV sets and God's power would pulsate through their TVs into them and raise them back to life.

According to this same vision, little children would receive an impartation of the Holy Spirit simply by placing their hands on their TV sets. God had really big plans for the future of TBN. "TBN will no longer be just a television network," Hinn said. "It will be an extension of heaven to earth."

Just then, Hinn claimed to be hearing the voice of God speak and began to relate what he was hearing. "The Lord just said to me these words. I'm hearing myself say them for the first time: 'TBN will not be only a Christian network. It will be an extension of heaven to the earth.' An extension. It'll be like a—like a tube from heaven that the earth can look at and say, 'I'm looking at heaven. I'm partaking of—of heaven. I'm getting connected to heaven through this TBN tube.' If I can say it, it will be heaven's signal to the earth. It will be as though heaven is transmitting and earth is receiving through that set. So if you want to go to heaven, you want to see heaven, you want to taste heaven, turn on that channel, because you will."

Since TBN insiders interpret Bible prophecy and their own dreams and visions as God's seal of approval on their work, it is the responsibility of all believers to study Bible prophecy and see if TBN fits into any acceptable scenario of the end times.

How has Bible prophecy been presented by the Crouches and TBN regulars over their thirty-six year history? Is there a consensus among them of the nearness of the return of the Lord and what role TBN plays? These are questions well worth examining to form any conclusions regarding their high-minded claims.

CHAPTER THREE

THE GREAT APOSTASY

BIBLE PROPHECY—SUBJECT TO CHANGE

In the early days of TBN, the idea of an imminent rapture set the tone of the network's eschatology (the study of last things). In fact, Paul and Jan Crouch would get excited any time world events signaled a warning that trouble was escalating in the Middle East. They would bring on their regular end-times experts. Besides Hal Lindsey, there were Doug Clark, Charles Taylor, Dr. Steuart McBirnie, and a host of other experts who would analyze current events to see where we were on the Armageddon clock. It was always about one minute to midnight, according to their estimations.

One particularly interesting *Praise the Lord* program featured Lindsey, Clark, and McBirnie hashing out whether the rapture would take place "pre-," "mid-," or "post-" Tribulation. It was a friendly discussion, yet Crouch always took the pre-trib position with his friend, Lindsey.

Up until around 1988, just about every Praise-a-thon focused on the imminent rapture of the Church as an incentive for people to call and get in on the final gathering of souls before it was too late.

"I have asked you this question a hundred times or more,"

Crouch wrote to his supporters in his January 1987 newsletter. "WILL YOU GO WITH JAN AND ME another mile? Will you hold our hands up another year? This could be the final one you know. This could be our 'Battle of the Bulge!'"[52]

In fact, the following year, 1988, Crouch was so confident that Jesus would return during the coming Feast of Trumpets or Rosh Hashanah, that TBN altered their regular programming during that Jewish feast on September 11–13, 1988, and played re-runs of pre-recorded shows that focused on the rapture.

"But to Christians curious about Bible prophecy," wrote William Alnor in his book, *Soothsayers of the Second Advent*, "it was also the target date on which Edgar C. Whisenant, a former NASA engineer, told the world that Christ would rapture the church into heaven."

Whisenant's book, *88 Reasons Why the Rapture Could Be in 1988*, had made an impression on the Crouches, which could also have contributed to Jan Crouch's subsequent disenchantment with the pre-trib rapture position.

Although Paul Crouch always held onto his belief in the soon return of Jesus, his wife Jan appeared to be going in a post-millennial direction. In the early 1990s she began what looked like a boycott of programs that focused on the traditional end-times views. Yet, when Bishop Earl Paulk and other anti-rapture guests would show up, Jan would be there and share their enthusiasm.

Anytime the subject of "Kingdom Now" doctrine would arise Jan would show her excitement about the view that Jesus would not return until the church had ruled over the earth for a thousand years.

On the other hand, Paul Crouch began expressing what is known as the "latter rain" or "manifest sons of God" doctrine that says that before Jesus returns, there would be a second Pentecost that would result in a final great revival that would herald the Lord's soon return. The Crouch home seemed divided on the subject of Bible prophecy.

But the possibility of an impending rapture made for good fundraising. In the January 1990 TBN newsletter, Paul Crouch wrote, "Beloved Partners, our world is changing dramatically...When you add all the natural disasters, the shaking of the Church to its very foundation, PLUS the great outpourings of the Spirit at home and abroad—WE WHO KNOW THE LORD realize that this is IT! The 1990s will be the last GREAT HARVEST of souls. And YOU and YOUR TBN are a vital part of this HARVEST...Jan and I depend on YOU to help keep this MIGHTY LIGHTHOUSE ON THE AIR!" (emphasis in original).[53]

Later that year, during the Fall 1990 Praise-a-thon, old time tent revivalist R. W. Schambach confirmed TBN's position that the 1990s was the final decade. "Get ready for the greatest move of God you have ever seen," Schambach thundered in his typical style. "This is the final decade! This is the countdown hour!"[54]

Benny Hinn also verified Paul Crouch's assertion that the rapture would occur in the 1990s. "Paul, I can say this," he said during the Fall 1990 Praise-a-thon, "Are you ready for this? We may have two years before the rapture...I'm going to show you scriptures tonight that are going to send goose bumps up and down your spine, up and down your legs and maybe in your brain...Can I be blunt with you? I don't know if we have two years left."[55]

Crouch was quick to grasp onto the revelation. "Benny's got me all excited," shouted Crouch. "He's going to open the scripture. Could it be that we only have two years left before the rapture of the church of Jesus Christ? I don't know, but I'm gonna be looking."

By the mid-1990s using the imminent rapture as an incentive for viewers to donate was losing its effect on TBN supporters. Crouch's exasperation began to show in 1992 when Hinn's prediction failed.

"I told Hal Lindsey the other day," Crouch lamented, "that if Jesus hasn't come by the year 2000, I'm holding he and Dr. McBirnie, all of them, personally responsible for this. It has to happen within the next few years or we misread the whole thing! I mean we gotta go back and reinterpret the whole thing."[56]

The disappointments in the delay of the Lord's return resulted in a new attitude on other Christian television networks as well. Phil Munsey, hosting a Cornerstone Network telethon, expressed his exasperation. "Now some of you are saying, 'Brother Munsey, you're saying that Jesus Christ is not going to come for another generation?' Yes! That's what I'm saying. Somebody say, 'Well my God, what if you're wrong?' Well, everybody else has been wrong for a long time. I'm gonna go on the other side."[57]

The apostle Peter prophesied about this change of attitude in the church in the last days. "Scoffers will come in the last days, walking according to their own lusts, and saying, 'Where is the promise of His coming? For since the fathers fell asleep, all things continue as they were from the beginning of creation'" (2 Peter 3:3–4).

After the disappointment of 1988 the idea of Jesus coming to establish his Kingdom gave way to TBN establishing the Kingdom for Him, a concept that started out as meaning to make converts but developed into a cry to take over the wealth and power and rulership of the planet. Quoting a verse that prophesied a future time of the millennial rule of Christ after His return, the headline of the March 1990 TBN newsletter read: "THE SAINTS SHALL TAKE THE KINGDOM. 'But the saints of the most high shall take the kingdom, and possess the kingdom for ever, even for ever and ever.' Daniel 7:18 KJV."

Crouch continued, "Sounds like FIGHTING words to me! Praise God, we are finally understanding that IF THIS KINGDOM IS GOING TO BE TAKEN we are going to have to DO IT in Jesus' name."[58]

To this day Paul Crouch wavers between the two views. He speaks of taking over the kingdoms of this world even while he's waiting for the King of kings to come back and take over where TBN leaves off. TBN bankrolled a movie about the battle of Armageddon called *Megiddo*, produced by the Crouches' second son Matthew Crouch and his company Gener8Xion Entertainment.

TBN's first end-times movie, *The Omega Code*, gave Matthew Crouch his start in Hollywood. And though both movies presented a contemporary timing of the Great Tribulation, the younger Crouch didn't share his father's view of Bible prophecy.

On one *Praise the Lord* program hosted by Matthew and his wife, Laurie, he told guest Kim Clement that he hopes Jesus doesn't come back soon because he has too much to do. Clement, who is Matt's personal prophet, told him that "we have a hundred years left to become that spotless bride."

Matthew expressed his views in an interview in the August 1999 issue of *Charisma* magazine: "Does Matt Crouch believe Jesus' return will happen soon, perhaps at the onset of the next millennium? 'No, I don't, and we are not trying to say that in the movie,' he said. 'I still have too much to do.'"[59]

Also on another *Praise the Lord* program Matthew took aim at prophecy teacher Jack Van Impe for using a prophetic speculation to get people to buy their books and videos. He called this tactic despicable, even though his father built his network by appealing to viewers to get in on the final harvest of souls before the Lord's return.

"I thought of the scripture about the wheat and the tares," Matthew said to Clement. "It's almost like the church, even on TBN, even on Christian television; we're all on the same team trying to win—It's like there's just a tearing right down the middle of mindsets that you either think it's doom and gloom and we're gonna be raptured out of this stinkin' place or we're gonna take it back for the kingdom of God."

"That's where I stand," Clement responded.

"Me too," said Matthew.[60]

That is a point well taken. He could have put it another way, is our citizenship in heaven or in the world?

"For our citizenship is in heaven, from which we also eagerly wait for the Savior, the Lord Jesus Christ" (Philippians 3:20).

Is the church at the time of Christ's Second Coming a scattered remnant of true believers or a united army of victorious warriors?

The letters to the churches addressed by Jesus in the book of Revelation best describe the visible church at the end of the age. Theologians have long pointed out that the seven churches not only reveal the churches that existed at the end of the first century when the apostle John wrote the book, but that they are a prophetic glimpse of church history from beginning to end.

Listed there are two faithful churches, the persecuted church at Smyrna and the church of Philadelphia that will be kept from the hour of trial which shall come upon the whole world, to test those who dwell on the earth.[61]

Jesus has a rebuke for four of the other churches that have a few faithful ones within, but as a whole these four churches hold false doctrines. Yet Jesus still counts them as the visible church because they name the name of Christ. The last of the seven is the one that has no redeemable value and is a peek at the last group that names the name of Christ. For this "church" Jesus has nothing good to say. That is the church of Laodicea.

Bible scholars have noted that with each church age represented by these seven churches, there is an overlap during the time one age fades away and the new one arises, although there are pockets of each of the seven throughout history. So during the time that the

Laodicean church rises to prominence, the true church of Philadelphia is losing influence.

The church of Philadelphia is not presented as some great ruling class of powerfully anointed Christians. Rather Jesus says she has "a little strength, have kept My word, and have not denied My name" (Rev. 3:8).

It would seem that the body of believers who escape the Great Tribulation is not a powerful force but one left with a "little strength." They have remained faithful to the Lord by accurately handling the Word of truth. They are not embarrassed to share in Christ's humiliation and suffering and walk humbly with their Lord.

Throughout the Gospels Jesus tells his followers that they are "the salt of the earth." Salt is something that gets sprinkled all over, not piled up in a lump. He also compares His followers to lights in the darkness. In this analogy, again the lights must be spread out. And after the Lord ascended into heaven after His resurrection, the book of Acts tells us that His disciples were scattered around.

"Therefore those who were scattered went everywhere preaching the Word" (Acts 8:4).

The Bible is consistent in showing that though true believers are one in Spirit, they are scattered geographically until that great day when He gathers them together.

"And He will send His angels with a great sound of a trumpet, and they will gather together His elect from the four winds, from one end of heaven to the other" (Matt 24:31).

The apostle Paul reiterates this view: "that in the dispensation of the fullness of the times He might gather together in one all things in Christ, both which are in heaven and which are on earth—in Him" (Eph. 1:10).

The church in the last days is clearly seen in the parable of the ten virgins in the twenty-fifth chapter of Matthew's Gospel. All ten virgins have lamps but only five of them have oil in their lamps, while the others do not. They needed the oil in order to light their lamps so they could see the coming of the bridegroom. The five with the lit lamps were watchful and living in anticipation of the coming of the bridegroom. The others were careless and obviously not anticipating that the bridegroom's coming was near.

In biblical symbolism the oil represents the indwelling Holy Spirit. The wise virgins were filled with the Spirit, although they too were given to sleep, much like the apostles when Jesus was about to be betrayed. The ministry of the Holy Spirit would be evident in the lives of the true remnant. He will direct the true church in sound doctrine and truth.

> However, when He, the Spirit of truth, has come, He will guide you into all truth; for He will not speak on His own authority, but whatever He hears He will speak; and He will tell you things to come. (John 16:13)

The virgins without oil in their lamps look like the others outwardly, but are not of the same Spirit. They are foolish and are not watchful and miss out on the wedding feast. Jesus must have had them in mind when He said, "The sons of the kingdom will be cast out into outer darkness" (Matt. 8:12).

What "kingdom" is Jesus referring to? Could it be the earthly/worldly one being built in His name?

If the five virgins with the oil are the ones that are kept from the hour of testing as is promised to the church of Philadelphia, then the unwise or foolish virgins that are left behind are summed up in the very last of the seven churches—the professing Christians who weren't watching and get left behind. They are professors—not possessors.

This is what Jesus thinks of them: "Because you say, 'I am rich, have become wealthy, and have need of nothing'—and do not know that you are wretched, miserable, poor, blind, and naked..." (Rev. 3:17).

So this final church is outwardly very wealthy in this world's riches but bankrupt when it comes to inner quality. A closer look at these foolish virgins is seen in the book of the Bible just before the book of Revelation—Jude.

Jude, the Lord's earthly brother, identified these professing Christians as those we would encounter from within the church. "For certain men have crept in unnoticed, who long ago were marked out for this condemnation" (Jude 4).

So these people that name the name of Christ would introduce false doctrine, turn grace into an excuse for lewdness, and indulge in sexual immorality. They would be noted for going on feelings, or what Jude compared to animal instincts (vs.10) and revile devils by their own authority. They would be greedy and prophesy falsely for profit like Balaam, serving their own selfish needs.

They also flatter each other to gain advantage and are very boastful of themselves. They walk after their own lusts and are complainers and grumblers. Jude says they defile the flesh, which is a difficult statement to understand, but it could refer to those who abuse their bodies with substance abuse or put other harmful things into their bodies, perhaps even things like silicone and animal collagen. They are also very sensual—going by the senses—and they cause division in the body of Christ.

During the time of the Great Tribulation, this church becomes what is referred to in the book of Revelation as the Great Whore. Her characteristics include the power to perform lying signs and wonders; she is drunk with the wine of her fornication, which means spiritual unfaithfulness. She is in bed with the world and conspires with kings and world leaders, who eventually turn on her. Her influence is worldwide and she exports her goods globally. Just before God lowers the boom on her judgment He commands true believers to come out of her. "Come out of her, my people, lest you share in her sins and lest you receive of her plagues" (Rev. 18:4).

Another name for her is Mystery Babylon, which is a revival of the old mythology that always opposed God's purposes, as she deceived the people with her sorceries. Not only does she have many craftsmen, but she also produces music of all kinds (see Rev. 18:22).

The church in Philadelphia bears the fruit of the Spirit and "have crucified the flesh with its passions and desires," according to the book of Galatians. The fruit in their lives is "love, joy, peace, longsuffering, kindness, goodness, faithfulness, gentleness, self-control" (Gal. 5:22–23).

Compare that to the list of the works of the flesh that characterize the church of Laodicea. "Now the works of the flesh are evident, which are: adultery, fornication, uncleanness, lewdness, idolatry, sorcery, hatred, contentions, jealousies, outbursts of wrath, selfish ambitions, dissentions, heresies, envy, murders, drunkenness, revelries, and the like" (Gal. 5:19–21).

THE GREAT APOSTASY

The change from the church of Philadelphia to the church of Laodicea is what the Bible refers to as the "great falling away" or the great apostasy.

"Let no one deceive you by any means; for that Day will not come unless the falling away comes first" (2 Thessalonians 2:3).

Historically, there has always been apostasy in Christendom. Therefore this great and final sign before the beginning of the Great Tribulation has to stand out from all the other heresies and cults of the last two thousand years. As with the other signs of the times that Jesus gave, like birth pangs, the ultimate fulfillment will be an extreme case compared to the similar signs leading up to it. Jesus said that in this world we will have tribulation and indeed we have, but the Great Tribulation will be a global condition that makes all other crises in history pale by comparison.

Conditions in the world are gearing up for the time that God pours out His wrath on a Christ-rejecting world. And the apostasy, in bed with the world, is also rising in power and global unity. God will allow them both to prosper and take root until the cup of His indignation is full and ready to be poured out.

CHAPTER FOUR

PROPONENTS OF A NEW PARADIGM

AQUARIAN CONSPIRACY REVISITED

Early in the decade of the 1980s, a book rose to the bestsellers list that frightened many Christian leaders and marked the birth of the world's awareness of the New Age movement. That book was *The Aquarian Conspiracy*, written by sociologist Marilyn Ferguson. It was instantly recognized by the church as a threat to God's truth and a force to be reckoned with.

The Aquarian Conspiracy came to be known as the bible of the New Agers and American Bookseller referred to the book as "the New Age watershed classic." It drew a line in the sand between "us" and "them"—true Christianity and the devil's counterfeit spirituality. The church at that time rightly discerned the New Age movement, as outlined in Ferguson's book, to be demonically inspired in preparation for the anticipated unveiling of the man of sin—the antichrist.

Ferguson identified this New Age movement as an unconscious conspiracy between people around the world whose souls were being transformed in preparation for the next evolutionary leap in humankind. The transformation would be complete when a critical mass of the new revolutionaries took the helm of all areas of life. This would then usher in a new age of peace and harmony on Mother Earth.

All areas of society needed to be changed to achieve the new era—education, politics, the arts, ethics and morals, and religion. Ferguson called the moment of entry into the new consciousness "the paradigm shift."

"New perspectives give birth to new historic ages," Ferguson explained. "Humankind has had many dramatic revolutions of understanding—great leaps, sudden liberation from old limits...A paradigm is a scheme for understanding and explaining certain aspects of reality...Usually at the point of crisis, someone has a great heretical idea. A powerful new insight explains the apparent contradictions. It introduces a new principle—a new perspective."

"New paradigms are nearly always received with coolness, even mockery and hostility," Ferguson continued. "The idea may appear bizarre, even fuzzy, at first because the discoverer made an intuitive leap and does not have all the data in place yet."[62]

She went on to explain that initially the paradigm shift is not usually recognized by everyone—old thinkers don't go along with it. But it becomes so pervasive in society that the children of the old order fall in line with it.

"But the new paradigm gains ascendance. A new generation recognizes its power. When a critical number of thinkers has accepted the new idea, a collective paradigm shift has occurred. Enough people have caught onto the new perspective, or have grown up with it, to form a consensus."[63]

It would appear that Ferguson's vision has indeed occurred in the world, to an extent. What she calls "the spirit of the age" has come into power in the lives of unbelievers around the globe. New Agers spoke often in the 1980s of a new perspective in the field of medicine, where Eastern mysticism would be joined with modern science. Now today holistic health is no longer considered quackery. Self-hypnosis is common and meditation and altered states of consciousness, under the banner of relaxation therapies, are no longer seen as suspect.

The New Age movement has made similar strides in the area of the arts. Hollywood has made the paradigm shift and now presents occultism and psychic phenomena as commonplace and no longer exclusively seen in sci-fi movies.

In other areas of society, New Age ideas of tolerance for homosexuality and other perversions are now in the mainstream. Vice departments in law enforcement are down-sized. Many perversions are now okay and accepted as alternate lifestyles.

The New Age movement has also achieved its goal in society through the feminist movement. Traditional roles of the genders are now a thing of the past. Marriage is becoming obsolete as now more babies are born out of wedlock than to married couples. The idea of family life has taken on the New Age idea of a variety of domestic situations that would be considered unacceptable in our parents' day.

All this just goes to show that what the Bible refers to as "the god of this world" is certainly in control of this world system. He has had his way in the world. But, is he having his way with the church as well?

CRITICAL MASS IN THE CHURCH

"There's about to be a wind from heaven that's about to blow," announced Phil Munsey from the stage of TBN's Conway Twitty auditorium in Nashville. "Everything that's been going that way—there's going to be a shift going on in the heavenlies. There's going to be a paradigm shift in the philosophies of men. Already now Mother

Earth is groaning in travail, laboring pains right now, ready to give birth to something big and something mighty and wonderful. And when that wind blows and what was once first and those will be last when it turns around, everybody will turn around and the last will be first."[64]

As Munsey heralded those words, TBN co-founder Jan Crouch jumped to her feet from her seat on the platform and clapped her hands and shouted.

"The church is about to make a quantum leap," Munsey continued. "Hear me! We are about to go from horse and buggy mindset. We're like a top right now. We're like a pressure cooker. We have been stuck for so long and everybody else has been making advancements in technology, in medicine, in every arena, but the church remains stuck in its same mindset with a big god inside of it."[65]

Munsey recognizes the strides the New Age has made in other areas of society, and apparently does not want the church to be left behind. And the TBN crowd cheered him on in his pep rally for the new paradigm.

Pastor and teacher, Joseph Chambers, rightly pointed out in his video production *Trinity Broadcast Network: Temple to the Gods & Goddesses* [*sic*], that TBN is at the helm of bringing the global church into a new religious paradigm—one that Marilyn Ferguson would approve of.

"A paradigm shift has occurred," said Chambers after playing the Phil Munsey clip. "There's no question but that this new mystery of iniquity is seeking to replace and supplant the mystery of godliness as revealed in 1 Timothy 3:16."[66]

Munsey's sermon was broadcast around the world to new believers and unsuspecting Christians who now await the next word from God by the mouth of the new "prophets." Christian television networks are the new paradigm's biggest tool for bringing about the critical mass necessary for achieving Munsey's religious New Age. This religious new age and the secular new age run on parallel tracks and will one day likely merge into the prophesied new world order.

"The capacity to spread the Gospel has multiplied a thousand times, possibly ten thousand times as to what it was thirty years ago," noted the late Walter Martin in the mid-1980s. "Praise God, but the capacity to activate and circulate evil has now multiplied correspondingly which means that you have more people propagating evil with more technology than you have Christians propagating it with the truth. That means the information explosion of misinformation that will avalanche the church probably between now and the year 2000."[67]

As it turns out, his words were prophetic. The church has been bombarded with an avalanche of false teaching over the past twenty years, which has laid the foundation for the new church, the false one, to prosper and take center stage.

The latest rhetoric that is consistently spouted by TBN guests and regulars is that God is doing a new thing and pouring out new wine that cannot be poured into old wineskins. The old wineskins are identified as the mainstream evangelical churches that they say are set in their ways and will be left out of the new thing God is doing.

"How many are ready to get into the new?" Kim Clement shouted to the TBN audience in early 2000. "How many are willing to break away from the old that's been shattered?"[68]

Later that year *Northwest Revival News*, an early computer newsletter of the prophetic movement in the church, released an issue of prophetic words about a coming "paradigm shift" in the church for the twenty-first century. James Goll, a so-called prophet and frequent guest on *Extreme Prophetic Television*, a program that airs on Canada's Miracle Channel, wrote an article called, "Paradigm Shifts for the 21st Century."

"As we approach the threshold of a new millennium," wrote Goll, "there will be a lot of shifting taking place in the church and the world. It is the time of completing unfinished business, a time of cleansing, and a time to get prepared for a spiritual churchquake to transpire in the life of what some prophetic voices call the Third Day Church."[69]

Some TBN prophets have spoken of a civil war in the church in which they intend to be the victors and take their rightful place in the world. Or as Ferguson pointed out, the new paradigm will be enemies of the old paradigm—those who won't go along with the new revelation.

The new paradigm church is waging a war against orthodoxy and poisoning the waters against the true church to paint them as a bunch of Pharisees that shouldn't be listened to. There is an obvious campaign being launched by the Crouches and other Christian media leaders to ostracize those who try to bring correction to the body of Christ. The critics are blackballed from the airwaves and compromisers who remain silent are rewarded and given places of importance and sometimes even their own television programs in exchange for looking the other way.

Viewers are unknowingly being conditioned to despise those who judge others' teachings and practices or who would dare to "touch God's anointed," a label given to Christian leaders who operate in the supernatural. The spirit behind the paradigm ensures that Christians put aside any critical thinking in order to ensure that the new way of thinking is not challenged. Those who get in the way are labeled "heresy hunters" or they are said to have religious spirits and are not to be taken seriously.

However, the spirit (or spirits) in control of the new paradigm church is a religious spirit, no doubt. It is the same spirit that is directing the secular world, using the same message, but dressed in religious jargon.

DOCTRINES OF DEVILS

What are some of the new ideas that the "spirit of the age" or the "god of this world" is bringing into the church with the help of Christian stations? How are they similar to the ideas that the same unclean spirit has brought into the secular world?

The most obvious theme common between the two is the idea of a man-powered new era of peace, prosperity, and dominion. The New Age movement got its name from the philosophy that in the age of Aquarius, when the Piscean age is faded away, they would achieve a united one-world system of harmony of the nations and put an end to war, hunger, ignorance, and pollution.

Similarly, the new church paradigm is preaching a new era also, a time when the children of God would hold their rightful place in the world by taking over all areas and having dominion over the world and the unbelievers. The vision is one where the righteous will inherit the land and take the wealth of the wicked to themselves. They would be masters in the area of the arts, education, the media, politics, and every other area of life. The kingdoms of this world would look to them for leadership. Or as the Word/Faith mantra goes, "We're the head and not the tail! We're above and not beneath!" All this would be accomplished before the return of Christ—they will have a kingdom without the King.

In the New Age system, the patriarchy steps aside and the matriarchy takes her rightful place of authority. The feminist movement, so empowered by New Age thinking, has accomplished this for the most part. The government has even put in place equal opportunity laws that force the corporate and political world to have hiring quotas for women.

In the new church system the women's movement is gaining ground in the same way. Women are now equally represented on the rolls of seminaries and are being ordained in the liberal churches as well as most, if not all, charismatic/Pentecostal denominations. The Bible teaching that women are not to be in authority over men in the family of God has been cast aside as a macho bigoted concept.

The New Age teaches that after the paradigm shift man becomes superhuman and evolves from Homosapian to Homonoeticus, which is the next evolutionary leap for humankind. The new man and woman out-surpasses the old order of man and has attained enlightenment, no longer trapped into the old way of thinking.

The new church paradigm speaks of the coming new breed of Christian who has become perfected so that he/she can walk in supernatural signs and wonders and speak with authority against all the principalities and powers that come against them. They refer to this "New Breed" as the manifestation of the sons of God, a term the Bible uses to describe the resurrected saints during the coming millennial rule of Christ on earth. They become the gods (with a little *g*) of the new era, more powerful than the apostles in the first century church.

The New Age paradigm promotes tolerance. Everybody has a little truth and should not reject anyone else's beliefs, other than those of intolerant people. Nobody is to be told they are wrong or their lifestyle is sinful. The only enemy of the New Age person is the true Christian who dares to present morals and ethics as black and white.

The ecumenical movement within the new church paradigm preaches unity in diversity, same as the New Age model. The cry of unity within this new church chooses to overlook false doctrines and accept any who name the name of Christ, whether they be Roman Catholic, Mormon, or Moonie. They say Christ can't come back for His bride until they become one and quit judging one another's beliefs. The solid Bible believers are seen as the enemy of the new church order. You can't turn on Christian television nowadays without hearing somebody slam biblical Christians, the old paradigm.

A blogger on a popular prophecy Web site summarized a popular idea of a civil war in the church that members of the New Apostolic Reformation often preach. He wrote:

In 1984 Bob Jones of the Kansas City false prophets, according to Wes Campbell[70] was told by God, "The Church is going to go into a time of deprivation."

After that time "God" was going to "throw a massive party." This was to be followed by a bloody civil war in the Church…They speak of the "blue coats" from the North fighting the "gray coats" from the South…the blue coats stand for the revelatory—the revelation, and the gray for gray matter—man's wisdom. Rick Joyner is convinced that the grays, whom he characterizes as "spiritually ruthless and cruel," must be "confronted and exposed and either converted or removed from their place of influence in the church." After the grays, who he says constitute "nearly half of the believers in the world today," are defeated, there will be "an entirely new definition of Christianity." As Joyner declared, "Believers and unbelievers alike will think that it is the end of Christianity as we know it, and it will be. Through this, the very definition of Christianity will be changed, for the better."

Fact is, if you alter "Christianity" so that it's no longer recognizable, then it's no longer Christianity![71]

A DARK SECRET

A recent book popularized by Oprah Winfrey is called *The Secret*, written by Rhonda Byrne. Cult expert Marcia Montenegro reviewed the book in the Spring 2007 *Midwest Christian Outreach Journal*. She traced the New Age beliefs in the book back to the Science of the Mind cults such as Ernest Holmes' Church of Religious Science and the Unity School of Christianity.

Montenegro pointed out that the god of New Thought is impersonal. "New Thought elevates man and brings down Jesus to being only a man who recognized His inner divinity (an attribute of all men) and knew how to use the hidden powers of the mind. This awareness of one's divinity is the 'spirit' of Christ or 'Christ Consciousness.'"[72]

In Holmes' biography, *Path of Discovery*, it is noted that he was "a central figure in the emerging spiritual consciousness of the twentieth century. His philosophy was not part of the 'old theology,' but rather one of freedom, fulfillment, joy, and unity with all life...Ernest believed that God is available to all of us, but that we must give up our limiting ideas and cultivate an awareness of the Presence within us if we are to experience the fullness of God."[73]

Even though Holmes was an open metaphysical cult leader, his biography notes that a "number of people [were] influenced by Ernest's teachings...Norman Vincent Peale, minister and author of *The Power of Positive Thinking*, studied Ernest's teachings from the time he was a young man, and the two men became friends many years later."[74]

Peale was mentor to Robert Schuller, pastor of the Crystal

Cathedral in Orange County, California. A larger-than-life bronze statue of Peale is on display in the cathedral across from a statue of the same magnitude of Schuller himself. Schuller, in turn, has mentored many other popular teachers including Bill Hybels of the church growth movement.

On a recent radio show called *Radio Liberty* with Dr. Stan Monteith, he spoke of the first edition of *The Secret* that was "channeled by Esther Hicks which Rhonda Byrne's film *The Secret* is based upon. The first edition was very much tied around the participation of a medium, a channeler, a psychic, an occultist...they have been the vehicles for the presence and the communication of a being called 'Abraham.'"[75] *The Secret* is based upon *The Law of Attraction*, another book by Hicks that is available in occult bookstores.

Dr. Stan's guest, Johanna Michaelsen, author of *The Beautiful Side of Evil*, recognizes that the ideas come from the occult, since before she came to a living relationship with Jesus Christ she was very much a part of the New Age movement.

"What is The Secret, which basically means the occult?" asked Dr. Stan.

"It's the Law of Attraction," Michaelsen replied, "that every vibrational thought you put out into the universe is responded to and answered. You picture what you want, you send and visualize and direct your energy to this thing and the universe will gladly and cheerfully and obligingly, like the genie in the magic lamp, move heaven and earth literally to answer your wish, to give you your command. And so they are presenting this now as the key thing."[76]

Knowing that these occult principles in *The Secret* are being espoused in the new paradigm church is cause for concern. TBN's favorite prophet, Kim Clement, in his recent book, *Call Me Crazy, But I'm Hearing God*, gave a new definition of prayer. "Prayer does not change things; prayer changes you and you change things," he wrote. "When prayer changes you and your perception of your circumstance, you can easily overcome. That's the way it works. That's the prophetic word in action."[77]

Clement even used the same terminology of the occultists and with the same basic meaning when he wrote: "When you know who you are in the eyes of God, there is an attraction toward you. People will be drawn to you because they are drawn to the light inside of you...The Law of Attraction will draw people to you. The Law of Attraction is the light of tomorrow—God."[78]

Clement says of this Law of Attraction: "It's God; unexplained, pure and unscathed by human vernacular."[79] Clement's ministry in Hollywood, California is called "Secrets." This could hardly be mere coincidence.

Other popular modern-day prophets have picked up on the terminology as well to attract a following. The disgraced tattooed evangelist, Todd Bentley, held an annual meeting in January 2008 of prophetic ministry called "The Secret Place VI," advertising the "DNA for miracles, signs and wonders."[80]

So, the Secret and the Law of Attraction came through channeling from the other side via naïve spiritual adventurers who influenced others both inside and outside the new paradigm church. However, these are not modern day ideas. The Law of Attraction can be traced in occult literature all the way back to the time of the pyramids.

At least that's the claim of Manly P. Hall, occult historian and author of the book *The Secret Destiny of America*, the primary source of conspiracy theories of early America and the alleged occult symbols on the dollar bill. In one of his lesser-known books published in 1922, *The Initiates of the Flame*, Hall reveals the identity of the ancient wisdom that has been passed down.

"The opportunity is now confronting the Western World. The knowledge of the ancients, the wisdom of the ages is knocking at the door and seeking those who will follow it," Hall writes. "The call is sounding, and those who love the Truth and think and care for the Light must join that band of servers who have for centuries dedicated themselves to the preservation of Truth…They are the keepers of the sacred Word, and the law of attraction draws them to all who love and live the Truth."[81]

Later in the book, Hall tracks those he calls the initiates of the flame back through history via various secret societies to the source of the Great Pyramid and its builders. He unveils the mystery that binds the ages together and is the capstone of the pyramid. He writes, "There must be no traitors to murder the builder this time. And Lucifer, the one rejected by man as the devil, is the one who must through the planet Mars send man the dynamic energy which man himself must transmute from the fire of passion to the flame of spirit. He then must take the tools of the craft and cut and polish his own being into the cap stone of the Universal Temple."[82]

A consistent theme of the new paradigm church is fire and flame. The secret place the new prophets speak of is not a location any Bible-believing Christian should mess with. The source of the flame is arcane and mysterious and will attract things believers will have a hard time breaking free of.

The church needs to heed the warnings of scripture to avoid the depths of Satan and doctrines of devils.

"For false christs and false prophets will rise and show great signs and wonders to deceive, if possible, even the elect" (Matthew 24:24).

To be forewarned is to be forearmed.

CHAPTER FIVE

REDEFINING CHURCH

WHO'S PERSECUTING WHO?

Whenever attempts have been made by concerned Christians to correct the false doctrine seen on TBN, Paul Crouch considers that persecution. He retaliates by blackballing them from appearing as guests on any TBN produced show. His favorite Bible verse to quote against these voices of reason is in the Gospel of John when Jesus said: "The time is coming that whoever kills you will think that he offers God service" (John 16:2b).

Yet the most violent and threatening gestures have come from Crouch, who has the attention of the entire world. The few dissenting voices that dare to speak out against TBN's heresies, false teachings, and spiritual extortion are prevented from responding to TBN with equal exposure to the masses. The ones with access to the world via satellite are the ones in command, not the few voices crying out in the wilderness.

The new paradigm church has declared war on the old Bible-believing paradigm. TBN uses the same tactics that the New Age movement uses to marginalize those who don't stick with the new program.

"A thorough reading of New Age literature will show that some new agers sanction the persecution of Christians," noted John Ankerberg and John Weldon in their booklet, "The Facts on the New Age Movement."[83] "They do so on the basis of the need to remove those who may refuse to accept or attempt to 'prevent' a spiritual uniting of humanity…If true globalism—or world unity—is eventually to be a reality, then by definition all dissenting voices must either be converted, silenced, or removed. That, of course, is the 'rub'—the New Age of love and harmony may have to be repressive for a time to usher in their version of peace on earth."

Those who hold true to biblical separation from false doctrine are an impediment to this ecumenical vision. The faithful ones become the enemies that must be wiped out or converted to the new way of thinking.

A term that has gained attention for the new paradigm is the Emergent Church that redefines church from a biblical-based system to one that is culturally based. Proponents appear to be uncomfortable with dogmatism, preferring gray to black and white. Although the Emergent Church gained popularity in academic circles with the writings of men like Brian McLaren and Tony Campolo, the real influences come out of the prophetic movement.

Emergent writer, Donald Miller coined the term "the new paradigm churches" in an article he wrote in 1996. Miller's Emergent book, *Blue Like Elvis*, helped to spread the message of discontentment with church life. Miller was a colleague of C. Peter Wagner, former co-teacher at Fuller Theological Seminary with the late John Wimber of the Signs and Wonders class back in the 1980s. Fuller is well-known for being on the leading edge of apostasy in Christian academia since it began denying biblical inerrancy.

Wagner began calling for a New Apostolic Reformation in which he envisioned a restoration of modern day apostles and prophets to be at the top of the hierarchy. He began referring to himself as an apostle and under the banner of the Apostolic Council of Prophetic Elders, he convinced others who saw themselves as apostles and prophets to acknowledge him and his new organization as their authority or covering. It has been this stream that is recognized by those who have high positions in Christian television. The Emergent stream of the same paradigm lives in a parallel universe in the non-charismatic church world where it is having a similar apostate influence.

Another one of Wagner's colleagues in the prophetic camp, John Eckhardt, wrote a book called *The Apostolic Church: God's Endtime Plan and Purpose for the Last Days*. Eckhardt spells out what the fate of those opposing this grand delusion would be. He writes:

> When you reject an apostolic company of believers, you are rejecting the Sender (Father, Son, Holy Spirit). They are identified with the Sender in such a way that accepting or rejecting the Lord is based on accepting or rejecting them…A delegation has power and authority delegated to them by the Sender. This causes an apostolic company of believers to operate in a higher level of power and authority than the average church. Their word and ministry will have the authority and power of the Sender…Cities and regions that reject apostolic churches will come under the judgment of God. To reject SENT ONES is the same as rejecting the SENDER. (emphasis in original)[84]

Another Wagner colleague on his *Council* is Cindy Jacobs. Jacobs heads up Generals International whose slogan is, "Achieving societal transformation through intercession and the prophetic." It has become popular to use military terms such as "generals" to convey a message of "comply or face the consequences."

This is seen also in "prophet" Rick Joyner's vision of "Civil War in the Church." He describes the coming church war as one that "will cause brother to turn against brother like we may have never witnessed in the church before…I do not believe that this one can now be stopped, or that the Lord wants it stopped. This battle must be fought. It is an opportunity to drive the accuser out of the church, and for the church to come into a unity that would otherwise be impossible…Believers and unbelievers alike will think that it is the end of Christianity as we know it, and it will be. Through this the very definition of Christianity will be changed, for the better. The church that emerges from what is coming will be full of unprecedented grace, truth, and unprecedented power."[85]

The "accuser" in the church he reveals in his thesis is one who would test the teachings of those in authority. He sees the enemy as those who "use doctrinal differences or other issues as justification for their attacks on their brothers."[86] He would consider this book, or any others that test all things if it involves the new hierarchy, as an opening shot in the battle for position in the new paradigm church.

John Arnott's wife Carol, in the heyday of the Toronto Revival, confirmed such war talk with a prophetic outburst. Tommy Tenney's online "GodChasers" newsletter reported the incident. It reported a meeting held at Rock Church in Baltimore back in 1997. It read:

> When Randy Clark announced his sermon title "The Making of a Warrior" the spirit fell powerfully on many people and especially on Carol Arnott. For about twenty minutes, while on the floor, she was slashing violently with a two-handed sword in her hands, her hands together as if holding a sword. After Randy finished his message, she got up and powerfully delivered the following prophecy…

"This is my sword," she said in first person as if from God. "My Golden sword…I am giving you my sword now and the old ways of doing things will not do. The old methods will not be acceptable to me anymore because I am doing a new thing…This new way is new and you must throw away the old ways of doing things and take up my sword because my sword is made of pure gold and is purer and is mighty."[87]

The same "GodChasers" newsletter, reporting about the same meeting in Baltimore, noted that another speaker, Marc Dupont, had a similar vision where "God was offering a golden pen and was willing to make a contract that would be signed in blood…Tommy Tenney felt we needed to seal everything by 'tying it to the altar.'"[88]

It appears that the old paradigm is not the one declaring war, but the power brokers of the new paradigm church do not feel they can co-exist. And they're willing to make blood oaths to accomplish their takeover.

TBN'S DUO

Two "prophetic" voices are often seen on Christian television to strengthen the new church paradigm and eradicate the old one or at least censor it. Kim Clement and Tommy Tenney have gained recognition as leaders of the new paradigm church.

"Prophet" Kim Clement is the founder of the Detroit-based "Kick Devil Butt Generation" ministries that was renamed "Warriors of the Millennium." He is now based in Hollywood, California using the name "Secrets" for his West Coast project. Clement stated his vision for his ministry: "I saw a vision of people that were wounded people, whom I would later call 'wounded warriors.' These 'wounded warriors' are people hurt by the religious system, unable to get healed because of isolation. These people loved God, yet didn't want to attend traditional church."[89]

Tommy Tenney is author of the charismatic bestseller, *The God Chasers.* "God Chasers Network is headed by Tommy and Jeannie Tenney," their Web page declares. "Their heart's desire is to see the presence and power of God fall—not just in churches, but on cities and communities all over the world."[90]

Tenney is best known for being the visiting speaker at Christian Tabernacle in Houston, Texas, back in 1997 where the preacher's pulpit was torn asunder by some unseen force. "I heard what sounded like a thunderclap echo through the building," Tenney wrote in *The God Chasers.* "The pastor was literally picked up and thrown backward about ten feet…When he went backward, the pulpit fell forward…It had split into two pieces almost as if lightning had hit it. At that instant the tangible terror of the presence of God filled that room…It was two and a half hours before [the pastor] could even get up, though—and even then the ushers had to carry him. Only his hand trembled slightly to give proof of life…The presence of God had hit that place like some kind of bomb."[91]

This story is reminiscent of a similar occurrence in the Old Testament, when God poured out judgment on the altar on the high places of Bethel:

> This is the sign which the LORD hath spoken; Behold, the altar shall be rent, and the ashes that are upon it shall be poured out. And it came to pass, when king Jeroboam heard the saying of the man of God, which had cried against the altar in Bethel, that he put forth his hand from the altar, saying, "Lay hold on him." And his hand, which he put forth against him, dried up, so that he could not pull it in again to him. The altar also was rent, and the ashes poured out from

the altar, according to the sign which the man of God had
given by the word of the LORD.[92]

Tenney presents the split pulpit as evidence that he and his
friends are endorsed by God. He memorialized this event years later
at a conference in Baltimore with the slogan that they "needed to seal
everything by 'tying it to the altar.'" But a split altar clearly shows that
if God were there, He was there in judgment, not pouring out a blessing. It is pathetic that today's sign-seekers saw this possible judgment
as a miracle that established Tenney as one of God's generals.

The god Tenney chases in his book, *The God Chasers*, is an
impersonal force that pervades the universe. "[God] is that 'particle'
in the atomic nucleus that nuclear physicists cannot see and can only
track," Tenney writes. "God is everywhere in everything. He is the
composite of everything, both the glue that hold the pieces of the
universe together and the pieces themselves."[93]

Certainly God holds the pieces of the universe together, but is
God part of the pieces themselves? Certainly not! God and His creation are not to be confused. Tenney's words sound like New Age
mystic, Matthew Fox, creator of the false teaching known as creation
spirituality. Fox was excommunicated from the Catholic Church for
bringing in his New Age influences and now is an ordained Episcopal priest. His new view of God, as is common with New Thought
cults, is known as Panentheism: "That we experience that the Divine
is in all things and all things are in the Divine."[94]

Some astute young believers have noticed the similarities between
Clement's teachings and that of the New Age movement. In defense
Clement writes in his doctrinal statement on his Web site: "My idea
that each person is born with a treasure in their spirit is mocked, and
I am accused of being a New Age prophet because I will NOT focus
on their sin but rather on their treasure."[95]

The belief in the innate goodness of man is a foundational tenet of the New Age movement, though it is contrary to biblical Christianity. Jesus testified, "There is no one good but God." The New Age movement and Kim Clement declare that man is merely ignorant of how good he truly is and to enlighten them to the divine within themselves will set them free.

During one of Clement's gatherings that aired live on TBN, a young woman came onto the platform flailing her arms wildly, dancing in circles, totally oblivious to everyone around her. Clement seemed amused and said, "There is a journey she's going on right now. It's a journey inside. She's running like hell to get inside to find out what God put inside of her is greater than what is on the outside."[96]

Clement shared his opinion of the nature of unsaved man (the opposite extreme of the Calvinist idea of the total depravity of man), when he explained why unsaved people are attracted to his meetings. "When they come in and there's a prophetic mantle which means you have vision…you're offering hope to that human being. He investigates himself and for the first time in his life finds that there's something good inside of him because the church and the gathering should be a place where you discover the greatness and the treasure of God that's inside of you, not the bad things."[97]

That's not the only area where Clement's New Age paradigm is at work. Clement and Tenney spell out their agenda on every appearance they make on TBN, among much adulation from hosts Matthew and Laurie Crouch.

RING OUT THE OLD; RING IN THE NEW

Tenney and Clement have gone to great lengths to create and destroy a straw man idea of the church. They rightly point out the evils in the liberal side of the professing church and criticize dead formality in the liturgical circles and create a false picture of a legalistic staid organized religious system, painting that as the norm—something easy to tear down. The same method of operation can be seen in the rhetoric of Catholic apologist Karl Keating, who refers to all non-Catholic Christians pejoratively as "Fundamentalists."

Clement and Tenney despise the dispensationalists that live in expectancy of the nearness of the rapture of the saints, and are on a campaign to discredit true Bible prophecy, to make room for the New Age idea of a Golden Age where the new breed church is influential. The old paradigm is any church tradition that does not go along with the new paradigm.

Their bad attitude against what they see as the old order of authority in the church fits in with TBN founder Paul Crouch's campaign against what he calls "heretic hunters." Crouch takes a jab at them on the air every chance he gets, no doubt to continually remind them that he's in charge of the airwaves and they should eat their hearts out.

"Heretic hunters, beware! You'll be running for cover before the end of the night," Crouch jeered,[98] as he proceeded with his regular routine of promoting false teachings and playing host to heretics.

Crouch passed his pet peeve against biblical Christianity down to his son, Matthew, who is taking the hate campaign even further than his father. Matthew Crouch describes his attitude as "anti-establishment," as he promotes Clement and Tenney as his partners in the spiritual hijacking of the church.

"Respectfully, you're talking about a wrecking ball going into Sunday mornings," the younger Crouch said to his guest, Tenney. "There's not a whole lot of churches in Southern California where I can think, 'OK, I'm gonna go and it's just going to get torn up and we're going to absolutely wreck'—You're talking about wrecking crew city!"[99]

Once the old church is wrecked, the new one can take over—a church that creates an atmosphere where supernatural manifestations, however wild, can flow freely. As Matthew Crouch puts it, "We don't care what the guy says; we want to feel the power of God."[100]

"All of a sudden, the definition popped into my head from the pages somewhere in 'God Chasers' that said that basically a hunger for God is a dissatisfaction with your present state," noted Matt Crouch on a *Praise* program. "That was the definition that clicked for me…I locked in on the book when I understood you say 'hunger is dissatisfaction'…I don't want to see the system the way it is because I'm dissatisfied with that."[101]

Paul Crouch came up with an appropriate name for the new paradigm church, "the Church of What's Happening Now."[102] Clement and Tenney's New Age version offers uncontrollable chaos as an antidote to what they perceive as stale church life.

THE PROPHET SPEAKS

Whenever Clement is a guest on TBN's *Praise the Lord* program, announcer Jim McClellan introduces him as "Prophet Kim Clement." Clement is laying down a new foundation in claiming to be a prophet in the sense of being a spokesperson for God. He has made himself an enemy of the body of Christ when he makes the claim that the church must be destroyed in order for him to begin a new one.

Clement likens himself to King David—the true king over God's people—and biblical Christian leaders are personified as King Saul—the people's choice. He writes:

King Saul and his choice soldiers (fresh from the best bible colleges) waved whimsical weapons; shouted silly slogans and simply waited for their hero to come...The trouble with leadership in the church today is they have embraced the power of "realistic" prognostication and rejected the futuristic powers of the prophetic...The old rejected order still survived because David had to grow up. Saul began to hate David. He eventually used the weapon that was intended for the enemy to wound his greatest warrior. This scenario is repeated in history time and time again. The old predictable order fights the new unpredictable one that begins to challenge the very forces of hell.[103]

Clement learned from divine revelation that he was to be a type of David, God's chosen. In a message on his official Web site, he relates what God supposedly told him after he asked God if he was to be a prophet like Elijah or John the Baptist:

The Spirit spoke to me and said: "Your stone will not hit the obvious, the distinguished nor the visible, but it will strike that which is hidden and unseen. You are like David and your ministry will always follow his life...Do you want to be accepted in the spiritual palace? If you do, you will never gather warriors, nor mighty men...Once you have gathered these mighty men, you will wait for the destruction of the present ruling forces—religious forces—that are attacking the 'generation of Davids.' These warriors will build another Zion to carry God's glory and bring forth Jesus with joy. Only then will you be anointed over Judah [praise]. David was anointed over the tribe of Judah first [for 7 ½ years] and then over Israel. So, you will first be recognized as ruler through the prophetic praise and worship that you produce, and then you will eventually have influence in Israel, [the Kingdom]." I fell to my knees and wept, recommitting myself to the journey God has sent me on to gather warriors for the new Millennium.[104]

These are strong words given the history of demented men such as Jim Jones and David Koresh. What makes it even more alarming is that Clement has the airwaves of TBN that reach around the world and with the Crouch endorsement he has scores of viewers hailing him as something great and the mouthpiece of God today. Referring to himself, after one of his prophesying to music rap sessions, he made an incredible boast to the cheers of the TBN crowd:

> God has raised up prophetic voices throughout the earth in order to bring forth his secrets to the church...What you heard tonight was not the voice of an eloquent person. What you heard tonight was the voice of God. Hello?!?[105]

He went on to lead the crowd in a chant for God to do something new:

> I don't know about you, but I think something different needs to happen. Something different needs to happen in the body of Christ. Something different needs to happen in the kingdom. I'm tired of the same old things happening over and over and over and over. I say, God, strike us down and give us something different. Give us something different. Give us something different today![106]

Clement is an undercover prophet of the New Age who has infiltrated the church to destroy it from within, and he shamelessly admits to that. Any who oppose him and TBN's vision is the enemy, but they are the ones who have rebelled against God and are inciting others to follow them in the rebellion. He is the "Saul"—man's choice, not those who speak up in defense of God's Word. It's just like the devil to make everything backward.

"There's no restraint," one evangelist said regarding the assault on the morals of our young people today. "'If it feels good, do it. Don't give us the Bible, that's being a Pharisee.' No! That's not being a Pharisee...Pharisees were people who taught as precepts of God the inventions of men, which is what they were doing. They're being taken captive because our society says, 'If it feels good do it.'"[107]

CONTEMPT FOR THE BIBLE

In Clement's meetings he whips the crowd into a frenzy with loud repetitious music that he claims is unrehearsed and performed impromptu as the spirit leads. The problem is that the mantras he leads his followers in chanting are silly mundane repetitions.

"I told my team we're not going to do any songs that we know anymore," Clement said. "And that was a very difficult thing 'cause you have to deny a lot because you get out there and you don't know what you're going to be doing next. That's the prophetic song. Song of the lord, we call it."[108]

Apparently, Clement thinks he is God's mouthpiece and he has no need to preach from the Bible. In fact, in all his TBN appearances so far, I've yet to see him open a Bible. He explains it this way:

> For those who don't think I know what the Bible is because we never open it: We don't open it because it's written across our heart. [109]
>
> We have music and I start saying stuff that I'm hearing in the heavens. We start repeating it and that becomes the

wisdom of God, which destroys the principalities that are present because they have to bow down to the wisdom of God.[110]

This is a very frightening trend that has been evolving at TBN for the past several years—an out-and-out assault on the Bible. When God's Word is anything that enters into the so-called prophet's head, soon the Bible itself no longer has any appeal. I never thought I'd see the day when the masses of people would set the written word aside in favor of the "latest word" from television preachers. But this is what Matthew Crouch is producing on the airwaves of TBN, and scores of people shockingly take it all to heart.

Paul Crouch has often opened interviews with professing "prophets" with the question, "Now what is God saying to us today?" Crouch has been doing that almost from day one, but he used to mean by that, "What's God showing you from His Word?" Now when the question is asked it's implied, "What extra-biblical revelation do you have today since the Bible was written thousands of years ago and is no longer relevant for today?"

The God Chaser himself, Tommy Tenney, put it this way:

A God chaser may be excited about some dusty truth…that passed in the path, and how long ago it was. But that's just the problem. How long ago was it? A true God chaser is not happy with just past truth; he must have present truth. God chasers don't want to just study from the moldy pages of what God has done; they're anxious to see what God is doing. There is a vast difference between present truth and past truth. I'm afraid that most of what the Church has studied is past truth, and very little of what we know is present truth.[111]

To get this new word, it is necessary to create an atmosphere in which the listeners shut their minds down and, as said before, the "prophet" enters into a trance.

Matthew Crouch, on a prime-time special *Praise* program in which TBN aired one of Clement's music fests, introduced him in a very strange way:

> Tonight is a prophetic service with Kim Clement. He is a prophet of the lord and he utilizes the atmosphere that's created by his ministry gift to speak to you and for God to speak through you...Kim's doing something right now. Throw your hands up in the air...A lot of time what that's doing is it's getting rid of what you would normally think to do. Getting rid of your mind; getting your flesh out of the way and absolutely going forward in the spirit. Call somebody. Say for the next two hours just shut your mind off. Turn your TV on and enter into a prophetic atmosphere where God can speak to you. Call a friend...you know what? Just shut your mind off, open your spirit and join into the prophetic meeting. It's right here on Praise the Lord![112]

This is the same direction you would get if you were in a New Age divination session. The Occult Dictionary defines this as "blank awareness," which is required for spirit communication. The person feels "that nothing is going on and yet one is awake; a state of consciousness in which one is not aware of anything in particular, and yet one is not asleep."[113] In this hypnotic state, one's reasoning powers are put on hold so that the audience cannot do what the Word of God tells them to do, i.e., "test the spirits."

The Bible is a Christian's only authority and ruler by which to measure any and all experiences. But this truth is being eroded away by Christian entertainment channels. One astute watchman put it this way: "If anything is contrary to scripture, it is wrong. If anything is the same as scripture, it is not needed. If anything goes beyond scripture, it has no authority."[114]

Those who hold to this biblical position are accused of worshipping the Bible. "Sometimes I think we almost fall into idolatry when we tend to worship the Word of our God more than the God of the Word," writes Tenney.[115] When Tenney reads the following scripture does he think it's referring to the "now-word" the God chasers are getting from the astral-plane, or the Holy Spirit inspired written Word of God?

> For the word of God is living and powerful, and sharper than any two-edged sword, piercing even to the division of soul and spirit, and of joints and marrow, and is a discerner of the thoughts and intents of the heart. (Heb. 4:12)

UNCONTROLLED CHAOS

The new paradigm church is not governed by scripture, which is seen as not relevant for today. The apostle Paul told the Corinthians to keep order in the assembly. Today he would be marked by the God chasers as boring and un-cool. Paul warns, "For God is not the author of confusion but of peace, as in all the churches of the saints" (1 Cor. 14:33).

During a riotous scene on TBN with Kim Clement on center stage, Matt and Laurie Crouch had this dialogue with guest Tenney in the studio:

"That is church, the way it's supposed to be," said Matt.

"All messed up!" his wife, Laurie responded.

"Absolutely chaotic at the hands of Kim Clement," Matthew

Crouch continued. "You walk in there and you see people going absolutely berserk in the presence of the lord and dancing. When you talked about losing dignity—there are people that lose their dignity that are hungry and passionate for praise and worship and they will show up at his meetings."

"I think he's got an anointing to kill religious spirits!" Tenney said.

"They are dead as a doornail, ha ha ha," Matthew nodded in agreement.

"When you do that, though, you elevate passion above program and that's when God moves," said Tenney, referring to the loud decibels of the music and the chaos in the crowd.

This passion that overtakes Clement comes out in his piano playing. He truly is a tremendous musician, as far as raw talent goes. In fact, his playing is so passionate that one gets the feeling that something paranormal is taking over and the crowd responds to him as they would to their favorite rock star.

"The blood that had come from my nails onto the keys that night, the way I played, was all over," Clement told the TBN viewers. "It was just amazing and that's the passion he's (Tenney) talking about. You can't be passionate without pain. Pain produces passion."[116]

And it gets stranger still. On an earlier program Clement described one of the times that the music took on a life of its own. "Last night we were prophesying on the instruments," Clement testified, "and suddenly this, altogether at the same time, all of my prophetic musicians started doing this eastern music. It was so weird; it's the weirdest thing you've ever heard. It was like, like somebody playing the things (imitates a snake charmer), and you could imagine a little snake coming out of a basket."[117]

Clement explained away the strange manifestation by figuring

God must be saying that he's going to be bringing revival to the Middle East.

Clement's electrifying music does seem to charge up the atmosphere, as he says. Once he had the crowd chant the same slogan over and over again and kept urging them to keep chanting. "Don't get tired of this," he shouted to the crowd. "We're singing into the atmosphere...I don't care what anybody thinks. God, we have no choice but to get away from our format and our rituals, our everyday mundane predictable events, even in church."[118]

"The reason we gather together in the house of God," Clement explains, "is so that we can drink the new wine, so we can get intoxicated and inebriated with the power of the holy spirit."[119]

Tenney warns the new paradigm church how to treat this new electrified atmosphere that they're able to create. "One of the first things God does when He 'turns on the power' in His Church," writes the God chaser, "is to bring back a respect for that power...It's not that we shouldn't come near it, 'use' it, or dwell in it. Just as an electrician is able to work around crackling 220-volt power lines with safety once he learns to respect the power of electricity."[120]

This power is what Tenney defines as bread from heaven and the words in the Bible are the crumbs of the past. "The next wave of true revival will bring waves of unchurched people into the House of Bread—people who have never darkened the door of a church in their lives. When they hear that there really is bread in the house, they will stream through our doors...Often we are so full and satisfied with other things that we insist on 'getting by' with our crumbs of the past...It is time for some of what I have politely termed 'divine discontent.'"[121]

The new church paradigm Tenney describes is for people who hate church and are hungry for metaphysical powers. These are the god chasers they seek who will make up this new millennial church—a church filled with unsaved, unrepentant, power chasers.

PSYCHIC PROPHET

Clement says these seekers are those that call psychic hotlines, seeking to look into an unknown future. He thinks the world's infatuation with the invisible world of the occult is a sign that God is drawing them to want spiritual experiences. Yet this worldly fascination with the occult is a mark of rebellion against the God of the Bible. Sign seekers scoff at the idea that they need to come to the Lord in repentance for their sins and yet Jesus said, "Those who are well have no need of a physician, but those who are sick. I did not come to call the righteous, but sinners, to repentance" (Mark 2:17).

Clement agrees with them that they are good within themselves and have no need for the Lord's atonement for their sins. He ridicules the old paradigm—the biblical one—for inviting sinners to repent.

> I'm telling you there's gonna be some ignoramuses coming to our meetings, the New Millennium Church, that's not focusing on the sin, and trying to force them to repent and make them afraid because they're going to go to hell and they're going to discover there's a glory, a beauty inside of me that only Christ can bring out by the power of his breath and his resurrection. And that's where the church is going; that's the New Millennium Church. And let me tell you something, it's gonna go out and when people come into their presence they're gonna be aware of something that they've never been aware of in their lives.[122]

As a postmodern trendsetter in the body of Christ, Clement has brought in converts who have come in through a different door other than through repentance towards Christ. Christian television has produced many false converts and has a challenge to keep them interested and their pledges coming in.

One secular historian, Scott Bartchy, director of the Center for the Study of Religion at UCLA, described the postmodern trend of the new spirituality:

> The phenomenon of cutting and pasting different beliefs to custom-make one's religion is more noticeable in Southern California. What I see happening here is that people are picking out the cherries that interest them, which generally in American culture means the glorification, the enhancement, of the individual...the new trend appeals because people can pick the pieces that make them feel good without having to make any changes. You are told that God loves you or that the spirit of the cosmos thinks favorably of you, or as some Hindu teachers love to say, "My goodness, all of you are recycled stardust." This is thrilling to hear, but you don't have to change a thing.[123]

This emerging church has all the traits of the Church of Laodicea that Jesus rebukes in the book of Revelation:

> "Because you say, 'I am rich, have become wealthy, and have need of nothing'—and do not know that you are wretched, miserable, poor, blind, and naked—I counsel you to buy from Me gold refined in the fire, that you may be rich; and white garments, that you may be clothed, that the shame of your nakedness may not be revealed; and anoint your eyes with eye salve, that you may see. As many as I love, I rebuke and chasten. Therefore be zealous and repent." (Rev. 3:17–19)

Jesus referred to those who seek after signs as being part of a "wicked generation." The unrepentant sign seekers want modern day magicians to satisfy their hunger for unexplained phenomena that titillate their itchy ears. Church growth proponents notice that too and see it as an opportunity to use the drawing power of the New Age magicians and psychics to attract a crowd.

Clement told the TBN viewers:

> The spirit of the Lord spoke to my heart and said to me, "Today the millions upon millions that are running to the psychics to the seers of this day, for triviality, for stupidity, for stuff that is insignificant and unimportant, they will go to them but end up at the prophet. They will end up in the house of the Lord...They're going to end up right in the house of the Lord, listening to the prophet of God, to the people of God that will predict to them, and tell them what their destiny is." You see that's what people are after, after all. They want to know what their destiny is...God says they're going to press a little bit further and they're going to ask for the prophets to come and tell them, "What do we have to do, where are we going to go, what is our future?"[124]

Bill Hamon, author of the book *Prophets and Personal Prophecy*, said that Clement has now outdistanced him in his prophetic abilities. Hamon says that Clement's gift has psychics green with envy.

"Kim Clement will tell you your name at times," Hamon told host Gary Greenwald on his TV program, *Saints Arise*. "He will tell you that a relative of yours was in prison in 1987, and that kind of very detailed words are going to really put the psychics to shame as God begins to speak to the prophets very specifically."[125]

One discernment minister pointed out how utterly ridiculous this

sort of chicanery is: "What do home addresses, descriptions of houses…
have to do with…true biblical prophecy? These are the things from
which parlor games and magical illusions are made. Tricks, psychic
gimmicks, and manipulation have no place in Christian ministry."[126]

Tenney agrees that the psychic seekers are their kind of people—
they just need to out-prognosticate the psychic hotlines to draw
them into the new paradigm church.

"I'm tired of the normal people," Tenney told the TBN audience. "There's never been a better day for an outbreak of God than
right now. If they're gonna watch for Sister Cleo, you know, there's
this flavor of the month in the psychics own, for a while it was
Dionne Warwick, and now it's Sister Cleo…If there's that much
demand that these people can buy all that time and do all that, you
know what that tells me? How incredible the level of hunger for the
spiritual and the supernatural is."[127]

Clement agreed with Tenney's assessment and interpreted the
worldly interest in the supernatural, as evidenced by the interest in
TV shows such as *X-Files*, as proof that God is pouring out His Spirit
upon Hollywood. This is one reason Clement moved his headquarters from Detroit to the major motion picture capital of the world.
"People are dying for it,"[128] Clement said, and he intends to give
them what they're after.

They concluded that the church must give the people what they
want. "And that's the reason psychics are so popular," noted elder
"prophet" Hamon, "because they are doing what the church should
be doing with the supernatural work of the Holy Ghost."[129]

The hunger for psychics is the same hunger that these New
Age God chasers want to see fostered in the church. "You can't tell
me they're not hungry for God," Tenney wrote in his book, *The
God Chasers*, "when they wear crystals around their necks, lay down
hundreds of dollars a day to listen to gurus, and call psychics to

the tune of billions of dollars per year. They're hungry to hear from something that's beyond themselves, something they are not hearing in the Church of today. The bottom line is that people are sick of church because the Church has been somewhat less than what the Book advertised! People want to connect with a higher power!"[130]

Clement spoke of his plan to give the higher-power-seekers what they want. He boasted of once prophesying over celebrities Steven Segal and Michael Jackson without using Christian terms.[131] He prophesied over Segal and then told him he was a prophet of the Lord. The Lord supposedly told Clement that it was quite okay not to identify himself as a Christian when prophesying over unbelievers.

The late Walter Martin, author of the book *Kingdom of the Cults*, shared his insights into the whole world of psychics and their clientele.

"You see what we're really facing as Christians right now is psychic phenomena as a substitute for faith," said Martin in a message entitled "Psychic Phenomena." "People who have abandoned faith in God and the Bible are turning to psychic phenomena and manifestation for what purpose? For the purpose of the conquest of fear and of death and of obtaining power here so that they can live."

"Why is psychic phenomena so attractive to so many people? Because it's unknown and it's exciting and because it's mysterious and because it displays power…It attracts people because it's unknown to you and whatever is unknown to you automatically attracts you. It's mysterious and people love an air of mystery…Why are people attracted to psychic phenomena in our day or any day?

1. It is unknown & exciting.
2. It is mysterious and appeals to our carnal nature.
3. It is a display of power outside of our capacity to control.
4. It is a substitute for hearing the voice of God.
5. It is a spiritual narcotic."[132]

Unfortunately, what Tenney and Clement are offering Christian television viewers is the same thing, dressed up in Christianized jargon. Failing to tell these seekers to repent from their quests in the realm of the occult will not set them free from the bondage that grips them. Like attracts like, and as Christian television operates in the occult more and more unsaved cultists will come to where the action is. The New Millennial Church will be filled to capacity—not with converts, but with sorcerers.

The New Testament message to these unbelievers is given in several places in the Bible. After Pentecost, the apostle Peter gave the first altar call. He said, "Repent therefore and be converted, that your sins may be blotted out, so that times of refreshing may come from the presence of the Lord" (Acts 3:19).

The new paradigm preachers leave out the "repent and be converted" part and appeal to the lost's desire to know secret things. Removing the call for repentance from the proclamation of the Gospel attacks the very core of how we approach God. The apostle John told us, "If we confess our sins, He is faithful and just to forgive us our sins and to cleanse us from all unrighteousness" (1 Jn. 1:9). Confession requires repentance. Without it we merely pay the Lord lip service and join the Laodicean church of self-reliance and self-fulfillment, a prime trait of the New Age movement.

DECEIVED AND BEING DECEIVED

The New Millennial Church has the devil's fingerprints all over it. Satan's nature is rebellion, and he is the prince of the power of the air—the realm of the occult where Tenney and Clement receive their inspiration. A major apologetics newsletter pointed out:

They ought to be exposed and held accountable for leading God's people away from a respect for the sufficiency of
Scripture, into Oda mystical land of "Christianized" for-
tune-telling. And there is a responsibility on the part of
believers as well. Christians need to forsake the enticing
inventions of these modern-day prophets and superstars.
They need to return to the safe and simple foundation of
Scripture—nothing more, nothing less, nothing else.[133]

The New Age movement is based on a latter day Gnosticism—
the cosmic illumination of the inner self which is accomplished after
a paradigm shift has occurred in which a person's worldview changes
from the old way of thinking to the new. Objective truth is replaced
with subjectivism.

The new paradigm church has been deceived by this spirit of the
age and is deceiving others and leading many foolish people into an
unholy alliance with the antichrist.

An old-time Baptist preacher, Gary Gilley, put it well:

The old gospel was about an offended God; the new gospel
is about a wounded us. The old gospel was about sin, the
new gospel is about needs; the old gospel was about our
need for righteousness, the new gospel is about our need for
fulfillment. The old gospel is offensive to those who are per-
ishing; the new gospel is attractive. Many are flocking to the
new gospel but it is altogether questionable how many are
actually being saved. What we need in our churches is not a
therapeutic, altered gospel that mirrors the spirit of the age,
but rather the courage to become relevant by preaching the
foolishness of the cross.[134]

CHAPTER SIX

THE ROOT OF ALL EVIL

G reed"—one of the seven deadly sins. The dictionary calls it: "An excessive desire to acquire or possess more than what one needs or deserves, especially with respect to material wealth."[135]

The last days' Church of Laodicea is marked as one full of greed and avarice. The church that Jesus is going to spew out of His mouth is rich in this world's goods. Jesus tells this church: "...you say, 'I am rich, have become wealthy, and have need of nothing'—and do not know that you are wretched, miserable, poor, blind, and naked—" (Rev. 3:17).

It has only been very recently that the accumulation of wealth has been interpreted as God's blessing on His people. One of the first preachers to popularize this notion in the 1960s was Reverend Ike. When he first burst on the scene he was immediately recognized as a religious phony. No Bible-believing Christian took him seriously. Yet even Ike is astounded at the chicanery of today's televangelists.

In the "letters to the editor" section of the January 1999 issue of *Charisma* magazine, Reverend Ike wrote in complaining of being villainized in an article written about a false prophet, Bernard Jordan. "My 'incessant financial appeals' are probably mid-range compared to the incessant financial appeals of every other church, minister, TV evangelists and those advertising products and events in *Charisma*."

Today the proverbial frog in the kettle is boiling away and the church is oblivious to the many scripture warnings against worldliness. The paradigm shift that has occurred is that of the church marrying the world and sharing its values. This new Laodicean church is indistinguishable from the world—the only difference is she attaches the name of "Christ" to all her worldly pursuits.

The church is warned over and over again in the epistles against the love of money, "the root of all evil." The apostle John warned:

Do not love the world or the things in the world. If anyone loves the world, the love of the Father is not in him. For all that is in the world—the lust of the flesh, the lust of the eyes, and the pride of life—is not of the Father but is of the world. (1 John 2:15–16)

And James, the Lord's brother, speaks out strongly to us against worldliness:

Adulterers and adulteresses! Do you not know that friendship with the world is enmity with God? Whoever therefore wants to be a friend of the world makes himself an enemy of God. (James 4:4)

When these verses are quoted to Paul and Jan Crouch, president and founders of the Trinity Broadcasting Network, the reaction is scorn and ridicule. They don't deal with the verses, but paint the opposition as people who think it's holy and desirable to be poor, something nobody is implying. In doing so they are actually ridiculing the ones who penned those verses.

Paul Crouch posed this question to his once favored fund-raiser: "We're supposed to be poor, aren't we, John Avanzini? We're supposed to have nothing. We're supposed to not have any wealth. We're supposed to be as poor as Job's turkey. Being poor is being godly in some people's minds. We're not to have wealth. Jesus, after all, Jesus was poor. We will have John explode that myth later tonight."[136]

God's Word gives us the balance—contentment. Jesus told some soldiers to "be content with your wages."[137] Paul told Timothy that "having food and clothing, with these we shall be content."[138] He also said that, "I have learned in whatever state I am, to be content."[139]

And the writer of Hebrews lets us know that God will supply our needs, not our greeds: "Let your conduct be without covetousness; be content with such things as you have. For He Himself has said, 'I will never leave you nor forsake you'" (Heb. 13:5).

Throughout scripture it has been shown again and again that when God's people, Israel, accumulated wealth and lived in prosperity they turned their back on God and brought about His wrath on themselves. History repeats itself as is seen prophetically in the last of the seven churches in Revelation. One writer of Proverbs recognized the needed balance:

> Two things I request of You, deprive me not before I die. Remove falsehood and lies far from me; give me neither poverty nor riches—feed me with the food allotted to me; lest I be full and deny You, And say, "Who is the Lord?" Or lest I be poor and steal, and profane the name of my God. (Prov. 30:7–9)

The ultimate personification of greed and the accumulation of wealth in a religious sense is seen very graphically in the Mother Harlot, Mystery Babylon at her destruction in the eighteenth chapter of

Revelation. After the removal of the restrainer at the beginning of the Great Tribulation, this one world "church" really comes into her own. She gains favor with the world and lives luxuriously, selling her merchandise of "gold and silver, precious stones and pearls, fine linen and purple, silk and scarlet, every kind of citron wood, every kind of object of ivory, every kind of object of most precious wood, bronze, iron, and marble and cinnamon and incense, fragrant oil and frankincense, wine and oil, fine flour and wheat, cattle and sheep, horses and chariots, and bodies and souls of men" (Rev. 18:12–13). When judgment comes and they lose it all in one day she cries and howls over the loss of her wealth because she has made wealth her god—that which she lives for.

This unified worldly harlot system also produces music and shines a lot of lights and operates in sorcery[140] in the name of Christ. So when Jan Crouch boasts of having more than a million lights covering the various TBN studios at Christmastime and Paul Crouch boasts that after the rapture "the antichrist" will pay TBN's electric bill, it's a cause for concern.

Prosperity gospel proponents repeatedly use a verse in the book of Proverbs as their own slogan for gathering riches for themselves. They say, "The wealth of the wicked is accumulated for the just." And they go about preaching to others to grab hold of it. The actual scripture verse is a proverb, not a promise to Christians. "A good man leaves an inheritance to his children's children, but the wealth of the sinner is stored up for the righteous" (Prov. 13:22). This is not a last days transfer of wealth as they boast, but in context it is an admonition to be wise with the use of our time.

"We have gotten along on pennies and nickels and dimes," Paul Crouch said, lamenting over having to get by on the widow's mite. "Brother John, it's changing. We are realizing that the wealth of this world does really belong to the people of God, the church of God. And we are hearing you and we are changing, but we have to move even faster."[141]

NO PITY FOR THE POOR

The problem with TBN and other televangelists' accumulation of wealth is that the bulk of it does not come from wealthy wicked people, but comes from poor Christian widows and children. The Crouches boast of being debt-free while telling their viewers to give to them before they pay their own bills. So while TBN insiders are living luxuriously, the ones who sent in their widow's mites are languishing in debt and can't pay their creditors.

"But thank you for the widow's mite too," acknowledged Crouch to his supporters. "The two dollars and the one dollar and the little children giving their allowances and their piggy banks."[142]

Studies have shown that it is the poor and needy who give the hardest. *Time Magazine* reported in an article entitled, "A New Way of Giving," the percentages of giving per household in America according to annual income. Those making under $10,000 per year gave the largest percentage, an average of 5.2 percent of their income, versus those making $75,000 to $99,999 per year who averaged 1.6 percent.[143]

Ole Anthony, president of the Trinity Foundation, a televangelism watchdog group out of Dallas, reported similar findings in regards to the field of Christian television supporters. "From our research, it seems this donor pool is an interesting mix," said Anthony. "About 60 percent are elderly women. Another 20 percent are what we call the 'moving pool,' or the 'desperation pool'— people who are themselves terminally ill or have a loved one who's sick. Among the rest are about 15 percent who are upper middle class who watch these televangelists because they want a justification for their greed."[144]

Targeting the ones who have the least to give, Crouch offered this admonition to compel them to send in their money: "'Well, I'm on the little fixed income. I can't afford'—you can't afford not to do something, to plant something. If you're going to obey the command of Jesus Christ and go into all the world and preach the Gospel, the only way many can do that is to send someone else…to give so that others can go."[145]

And yet the Bible admonishes us to give as we are prospered, not under compulsion: "On the first day of the week let each one of you lay something aside, storing up as he may prosper, that there be no collections when I come" (1 Cor. 16:2). And again: "So let each one give as he purposes in his heart, not grudgingly or of necessity; for God loves a cheerful giver" (2 Cor. 9:7).

Certainly even the poor Christian will give to others in more need than themselves because the Spirit of God certainly puts generosity into the hearts of His children. But for a billion-dollar organization to take advantage of the fact that Christians are givers and target the needy as they themselves live in the lap of luxury is an abomination. The Bible declares:

> He who oppresses the poor to increase his riches, And he who gives to the rich, will surely come to poverty. (Prov. 22:16)

So if the needy give to the rich, rather than receiving the hundredfold return TBN promises to their viewers, they end up deeper into poverty.

In contrast to TBN's willingness to take the last penny from a poor person, the founder of World Challenge ministries, David Wilkerson, wrote this to his supporters. "We pray God will move on those who are able to help, but I want to say to every widow and retired person on a very limited income; please do not feel obligated or pressured. Do not send us any money that you need for food or personal bills. God will meet our needs from those who are able and willing to give. This also goes for single mothers and for any unemployed or poor family. We will send you our message without cost. Just pray for us."[146]

I'll never forget a word of wisdom I learned from the late Walter Martin, author of *The Kingdom of the Cults*. He said. "You'll know a wolf in sheep's clothing by its diet. A wolf eats sheep."

TBN utilizes self-professed "prophetess" Juanita Bynum in their Praise-a-Thons on a regular basis. She is an embarrassment to Christian womanhood. Every time she raises money, she fleeces the sheep and offends anyone with discernment the size of a pea. She has recently filed for divorce from her second husband after they made a scene in a parking lot.[147] One example of spiritual extortion was done during TBN's fundraiser in November 2003. After trying to get people to call in with a pledge for her anointed handkerchiefs and berating the viewers for hours to give till it hurts, she made this plea:

> You watching me in the Television-land and you say, "All I got is $900." But I hear the Lord say, "I double-dare people that are watching me right now. This one is for you. I double-dare you to empty your checking account. If you got $79.36—empty it out! Empty it out at the voice of the prophet. If you got $736.19—if you in this audience right now"—You're all looking at me like I'm crazy. You looking at me like I've got one off. Oh Jesus! "If you got $79.36—I

double-dare you to write your last check and declare your
bank account empty," because God said…"when you give
him your last" he multiplies.[148]

What a shameful display of con-artistry, claiming to be a prophet
of God and telling people to give her the last of their money in order
to magically get more money for her to help herself to. (At times like
this I wish the old custom of tar and feathering shysters and putting
them in open shame was still in fashion.)

Another regular female money-grubbing preacher is Paula White
who is one of the televangelists on Senator Grassley's hit list. She too
just went through a messy divorce from her husband, pastor Randy
White, which devastated their congregation at the Church Without
Walls in Florida. She has a proven record at TBN for making the
phones ring off the hook for people she convinces must call in a
pledge in order to have their prayers answered.

Several years ago, White was a speaker at the *Charisma* Women's
Conference in Daytona Beach that was carried live on Sky Angel.
She led the six thousand women attending into a wanton display of
witchery that was hard to even look at. While screaming and jumping up and down like a voodoo priestess, White shouted to women
who were pouring out water into a barrel at the front of the platform
while others jumped up and down and spun around like snakes in
the bottom of a pit. She screeched:

> You're pregnant! You're pregnant with a promise. You're preg-
> nant with destiny; you're pregnant to be the head and not the
> tail. You're pregnant to possess the gates of your enemy…
> Somebody shout I'm pregnant! [White breaks out in gut-
> tural tongues while jumping.] Somebody's water just broke.
> Somebody's having some strong contractions right now!…

I'm not going to settle for a cup when God has promised me the whole well!…Devil, I'm not gonna compromise. Not just a cup; not just a cup…The fire of God is being poured out. See you're giving birth right now. Your water's already broke. You have the contraction. Push! Push! Push! [149]

Women in the crowd looked like they were in pain and bearing down as if giving birth. It was a shameful scene. This is just one of many shameful acts Paula White performs under the guise of being anointed by the Holy Spirit. She brings such shenanigans to just about every one of TBN's Praise-a-thons. She finds a way to use these dramatics to take an offering.

On one Praise-a-Thon, John Avanzini pointed out to Paul Crouch how easy it is to take up big offerings in the locations that get TBN. "You can tell as soon as you start speaking if that signal's in that area or not," Avanzini greedily bragged. "There's just not a flow unless that signal's in that city. But where the signal is in the city, the churches are easy. The people are loose. They receive revelation. You know, most places, really, you have to spend most of your time, if you're going to bring a revelation, you spend most of your time just trying to get them to receive basic principles." [150] The basic principles of the Seed-Faith lie is what he was referring to.

But, TBN's signal apparently doesn't do the trick everywhere. Paul Crouch once lamented that Europeans don't cough up the dough. "God is giving Europe time," Crouch said in disgust. "There is no harder, colder, more disinterested place on earth in the things of God. Not Eastern, but Western Europe…You can't get the people in Italy to give a dime to Christian television…They won't give. Even the Catholic Church suffers over there." [151]

TBN discourages personal evangelism, which is the commanded in scripture. Instead, viewers are encouraged to tell others about

TBN where the professionals can then give the Gospel on behalf of the supporters. If they give money to TBN for them to "reach out to the whole wide world," they've fulfilled their obligation to witness.

By TBN's standards those who live within humble means are not qualified to share the Gospel themselves because only the rich will be successful at it. The Crouches lift TBN up as God's end-times voice for spreading the Gospel and the millions of dollars they take in is the God-ordained fuel that runs the machine. "Oh, here comes the critics," Paul Crouch moaned. "Here comes the pitch. Crouch is after your money. Yes, I am! Hear it, devil! Hear it, press! Hear it, everybody! We're after money—for one reason—that this voice can be amplified a million more times. That this Gospel will be preached in the world."[152]

A good illustration of TBN's self-delusion that it takes lots of money to fulfill the Great Commission was revealed, perhaps unintentionally, by master manipulator, John Avanzini.

"Poverty can make your word be ignored," Avanzini taught on his now canceled[153] TBN-sponsored program, *Principles of Biblical Economics*. "You want to talk about a blessing. It's a blessing whenever you start to tell somebody how to get saved and they sit down and they want to hear it. It's quite something else when they look at you and say, 'Man, I don't want what you got. Are you saved? Wow, let me tell you something. I don't want to live like you live and have to drive around like you drive around.' Listen to it, your words are not heard when you walk around in insufficiency, when you walk in poverty."[154]

He concludes that the poor are second-class citizens in God's kingdom. "Child of God," Avanzini said to the TBN viewers, "our words have to be heard if we're going to be effective Christians. And one of the curses of poverty is, no one wants to listen to you."[155]

"Now, I can get a call from somebody, 'You know, brother John, I want to tell you that I don't think it's right to be preaching about money and blah, blah, blah, blah, blah. You know, I don't have any money and I'm getting along fine.' I'm not going to listen to that very long. But you let somebody call me up. You let somebody of import—you let a businessman call me up and say, 'Brother John, I want to tell you how God has blessed me and I want to put some finances into the kingdom of God.' I'll listen to that man. You'll listen to that man, too."[156]

Avanzini went on to explain how the big donors who support TBN are given favorable treatment over the poverty-stricken people who give little out of their want.

"And that person came in and they met him at the door and they were glad to see him and they walked him through the building and they showed him everything. Well, why doesn't everyone get that treatment that comes to the studio? Well, he was a giver. He gave to Trinity Broadcasting. He was one of the partners, so there was room for him when he came in. I don't think there was anyone in the room ever met him before, but room was established for him. It makes a place for him, see?"[157]

Yet the Bible teaches that "there is no partiality with God." TBN gives special treatment to the rich, which is in stark contrast to what the Bible says our attitude should be towards the poor:

My brethren, do not hold the faith of our Lord Jesus Christ, the Lord of glory, with partiality. For if there should come into your assembly a man with gold rings, in fine apparel, and there should also come in a poor man in filthy clothes, and you pay attention to the one wearing the fine clothes and say to him, "You sit here in a good place," and say to the poor man, "You stand there," or, "Sit here at my footstool," have you not shown partiality among yourselves, and become judges with evil thoughts? (James 2:1–3)

TBN founder Paul Crouch takes that a step further. Those who don't give to them will be the slaves of the ones who give. "Those of us who do give are going to get all the reward," Crouch boasted, while the TBN regulars stood behind him in agreement. "We're gonna get it all. They're going to be waitin' on us, boy. They're going to be washing our feet. They're going to be bringing you your late night TV snack dinner. They're going to be waiting on us in heaven, yes. You laugh, but that's absolutely true."[158]

Jan Crouch once spoke up for the poor folks and justified TBN's right to plunder them in the same breath. "The Lord just spoke to my heart something so sweet," she said during a "Macedonian Call" fund-raiser. "I thought, Lord these people are so poor (those living in Central America who were being asked to support TBN). And the Lord just spoke to me; 'I don't judge wealth of my people by what they have.' The Lord spoke to me; 'I judge wealth of my people by what they give.' The wealthiest people in God's eyes in the world can live in a hovel. And that's what we all want to be—wealthy in God's eyes…Isn't that sweet? I was so blessed, then I realized that a little grandma could be the wealthiest person living on the face of the earth, somewhere in Africa in a little grass hut, she had given her all and she is wealthy."[159]

Jesus had harsh words for those who fleece the flock and target the needy:

> Woe to you, scribes and Pharisees, hypocrites! For you devour widows' houses, and for a pretense make long prayers. Therefore you will receive greater condemnation. (Matt. 23:14)

THE RAISE-A-THONS

Twice a year, in November and April, TBN conducts one-week long fund-raisers they call the Praise-a-thon. Each day of the week they focus on a different aspect of the operation for viewers to pledge to. One day will be for satellite expenses and another for the budget of the nightly *Praise the Lord* program shown on prime time. The other days include budgets for building new stations, producing motion pictures, and general operating expenses.

In 1991, TBN conducted an emergency Praise-a-thon in the summer they gave the name, "The Macedonian Call." Paul Crouch insisted that it was a one-shot deal to raise money to plant a station in Macedonia. However, it must have worked out well for TBN because the "Macedonian Call" mini Praise-a-thon has been going on every summer since.

It's only been in the last couple of years that TBN has run excerpts from the Praise-a-thons sporadically over the year during the *Praise the Lord* time slot to keep the money coming in. So what started out as a semiannual event is now a much more frequent appeal for funds.

The late Larry Thomas, publisher of *The Inkhorn*, noted that the Praise-a-thons are "a lot more 'raisin' than 'praisin,'" and renamed the fund-raisers the "Raise-a-thons."[160] What "praisin" that is seen in the Raise-a-Thons is a tired mix of the same handful of musical regulars, singing the same songs they've been singing on TBN for over a decade. Walt Mills will sing "Ain't Got Time For You Devil" for the umpteenth time. Then Mike Purkey will belt out "Sweet Beulah Land," while lumbering back and forth, and Vern Jackson will comply with Jan's request for "Hello, Momma." Betty Jean Robinson might do twenty rounds of "He is Jehovah," while Candi Staton-Sussewell and Karen Wheaton go over their small repertoire. It's easier to watch the show on video so you can fast-forward through the music. The main function of the music is to move people to the telephones to call in their pledges since the phones don't ring while preaching is going on.

The Praise-a-thons employ the pressure tactics of TBN's more convincing prosperity teachers who are gifted at twisting scriptures to pressure viewers into giving till it hurts. They utilize a false teaching, known as the prosperity gospel, as a catalyst to convince donors that they must give to get.

The prosperity message encourages people to value materialism and use the so-called principle of Seed-Faith giving to reap a material harvest of wealth. This false teaching was made popular by Oral Roberts, a has-been faith healer who built his failing ministry upon its principles. In his book, *Miracle of Seed-Faith*, Roberts tells how God showed him that the farmer could not reap a harvest unless he first sowed some seed. Misusing the scripture, "whatsoever a man soweth, that shall he also reap," Roberts concluded that if you want answered prayer, you must sow a seed of faith to obtain God's favor.

So building off that principle, the Praise-a-thon's message is that in order to get rich or healed or your loved ones saved, you must sow a financial seed in order to obtain the desired results. The "give to get" mentality is promoted as a solid "Christian" value, though that attitude is consistently denigrated in the New Testament.

And one need not sow a financial seed for only money in return. As TBN fund-raising preacher, Mark Chironna says, "Some of you, you're sowing for a promotion. Some of you, you're sowing for a business contract." And John Avanzini successfully sowed financial seed for husbands for his two unlovely daughters. He told the TBN viewers how he and his wife desperately prayed for one of their daughters who had a condition that prevented her from growing hair on her head. How could they find a husband for her? They sowed a financial seed and God brought her a husband who had had polio as a child and walked with a limp. Avanzini boasted, "Cueball married Gimp!"[161]

Walter Martin, the original Bible-Answer-Man, agitated by the blab-it-and-grab-it philosophy seen on TBN once said, "The Bible tells you, you can demand of God whatever you want by faith and if God wants to give it to you He will. And if He doesn't want to give it to you, He won't because God is sovereign over the universe and not men."[162]

In the Sermon on the Mount, Jesus said, "But when you do a charitable deed, do not let your left hand know what your right hand is doing" (Matt. 6:3). And the apostle Paul warned that "the love of money is a root of all kinds of evil, for which some have strayed from the faith in their greediness, and pierced themselves through with many sorrows" (1 Tim. 6:10). These are strong words against those who would give you a formula for donating money in order to obtain wealth.

GAIN BY FALSE PROMISES

TBN promises the donors a hundredfold return on their investment. This teaching has gone through an evolution of meaning in the last ten years or so that they've been promoting the idea.

The first Praise-a-thon to push the hundredfold heresy was in the Fall of 1990. John Avanzini, founder of God's Debt-Free Army in Hurst, Texas, set the tone for the fund-raiser with the revelation that he was getting a now-word from God that would bless all who would grab hold of it.

Avanzini is a shifty-looking character from whom few people would be comfortable buying a used car. He sometimes wears a tie with dollar signs in the design and wears gold and diamond rings and a Rolex on one wrist and a gold bracelet on the other.[163]

He has a knack of dramatizing everything that he says as if he's coming up with something profound, but what comes out of his mouth is double-talk and hype. "I'm usually not allowed to speak about this," said Avanzini to the TBN audience on the opening day of the Fall 1990 Praise-a-thon. "God only tells me at certain times that I can. Many times I've been asked to tell this story, but I can't tell it unless God gives the clearance to...I really feel God speaking and saying, 'I want this voice in the earth.'"

Avanzini went on to recall a story of how he tried for years to join the ministry of televangelist Morris Cerullo, a con artist who was banned from British television. Wikipedia reports that "In 1991, British authorities suspended the license of a satellite station for broadcasting the program, *Victory with Morris Cerullo*. In 1999, the Christian Channel, a UK cable channel, broadcast an advertisement for one of Cerullo's European rallies which claimed that 'Satanic hordes' had 'occupied the principal palaces of power.' As a result, the channel was fined £20,000 for breaching advertising codes requiring political impartiality, for denigrating other religious beliefs, for potentially frightening viewers, and for making statements prejudicial of 'respect for human dignity.'"[164]

[This author attended one of Cerullo's meetings in Philadelphia and caught him faking a healing by bringing up a man from the audience with an oxygen tank who had written to him, telling him about how God had healed him. The man agreed to come and re-enact his healing to promote faith in the viewers, and Cerullo put on a show jumping up and down with the tank pretending that the miracle had just occurred.[165]]

Finally Avanzini got the opportunity to accompany Cerullo to his crusade in Abba, Nigeria. "When I came into Abba, Nigeria," Avanzini said, "the meeting was already underway...eighteen hundred black African leaders in that meeting, and as I came into that room all of a sudden something hit me and I thought, 'My goodness, it's hot in that room,' and I stepped back out of the building and I realized that there was something there that I had never ever experienced before."[166]

He told how God had supposedly appeared to him in his African hotel room and commissioned him to teach "God's economics." He went to the Morris Cerullo crusade the following day with instructions from God "to speak a hundredfold increase over that offering that it will be multiplied back to the giver a hundredfold!"

"I told them how the offering would be and they began to pass around two little bowls that they had with about two thousand leaders now in the room. Within one row the bowls were full…they started taking the offering with the pillowcases…and money was falling out of the balcony…and finally Dr. Cerullo stood up and he said, 'Stop the giving…' And I began to pray. I felt something hitting me and I looked up and the people were throwing money. Money was being thrown over the top of their heads."

[It is hard to imagine Morris Cerullo yelling, "Stop the giving," when the entire thrust of his ministry seems to be focused on the collection plate.]

Then Avanzini told the TBN audience that this was a lucky day for them. God was telling him to speak the hundredfold over their pledge slips. "At first, you know Jan Crouch has asked me a dozen times to speak the hundredfold message and I have to say, 'Jan, anything else, but God is just not letting me do it.' But tonight I feel it with all of my heart and soul. I'm going to speak the hundredfold increase tonight."

Apparently God has let him do it for every Praise-a-thon since. It must have generated a huge response because TBN got a record pledge total during that Fall 1990 fund-raiser. At the end of the program that night, Avanzini followed through on his promise. The entire prayer consisted of three sentences:

Father, we thank you that there's more than enough. We know the devil's a liar. Lord in the name of Jesus and in the power of your revelation we speak in the name of Jesus be multiplied hundredfold in Jesus' name, Amen.

God does reward His children for their generosity, but as He said, "hoping for nothing in return." As soon as a selfish motive is introduced into a Christian's giving, that actually prevents the blessing from occurring. TBN is robbing people of their reward when they encourage greed. And exhorting people to eagerly pursue riches sets them up for a fall. The apostle Paul put it this way:

But those who desire to be rich fall into temptation and a snare, and into many foolish and harmful lusts which drown men in destruction and perdition. (1 Tim. 6:9)

The poor donors who are looking for a financial blessing after paying TBN instead of their creditors have believed TBN's preachers that they will become rich because it is their right as a child of God. They want to cash in on the "great end-time wealth transfer" that Avanzini promised them.

"It would be nothing for God to give a hundred thousand dollars to a person," Avanzini told his desperate TV audience. "Why, a bank could do that; a lottery could do that and greater than a lottery has come. His name is Jesus and he can give us anything that the world could do, he would do."[167] In other messages he has compared God to other industrial giants claiming, "a greater than General Motors is come,"[168] "a greater than Ford Motor is come,"[169] "a greater than Citibank has come."[170]

It is a known fact that the biggest buyers of lottery tickets are the ones who can least afford them but are hoping for that one lucky windfall. This is the same measure of desperation that drives many of TBN's donors to listen to the talk of giving to get. This is also why it carries over well into the third world nations who look at Americans and desire what we have. They're made to believe that if they do what we do, they'll get what we got. Contrary to some critics of the prosperity gospel who say it wouldn't fly in the third world, it does fly—right in the face of God Almighty!

"It is a common characteristic of false teachers to have false promises," Pastor Greg Laurie told his congregation at Harvest Christian Fellowship in Riverside, California. (Laurie's Harvest Crusades air regularly on the Trinity Broadcasting Network, but he won't be heard speaking this way on that network.) "They promise that God will prosper you. 'Oh,' they say, 'if you will send in your gift right now we will pray the hundredfold blessing upon you.' You've seen these guys—'God's revealed to me he's going to give a hundredfold blessing, so if you sow $10 he'll give you the hundredfold blessing and multiply it. If you sow a hundred you'll get even more.' Interesting, though, 'If God's going to give you this blessing, first you have to give to me,' the false teachers say. It's a false message because you should never give to get because it's a wrong motive, going back to Cain."[171]

CHAPTER SEVEN

SPIRITUAL EXTORTION

Another one of TBN's favorite money preachers is R. W. Schambach, a loud shouting preacher who learned the trade from 1950s circuit riding faith healer, A. A. Allen. Schambach intersperses stories of miraculous signs and wonders from the old days into his current messages. He tells stories of seeing limbs grow back on amputees and of one four-year-old child who was born with twenty-six major diseases—blind, deaf, dumb, with tongue hanging out. He was crippled and deformed and had no feet—just clubs, and no sex organs, but was miraculously restored to normal at an A. A. Allen meeting,[172] Schambach testified during a TBN fundraiser.

Yet during the Fall 1990 Praise-A-thon Schambach appeared frustrated while preaching about signs and wonders and shouted, "Today we talk more about power than producing the power. If you have the power you don't have to talk about it, all you got to do is demonstrate it. The more we talk about it is the evidence we ain't got it, and that's all we been doing for ten years, and we been trying to force God to do miracles."

Schambach went on from there talking about more signs and wonders from his glory days while insisting, "I want you to know the church is going out in a blaze of glory. We're going out in a double portion fashion. I believe we're going to see more going out than what was originated in the book of Acts. Get ready for the greatest move of God you have ever seen...This is the final decade. This is the countdown hour...This is the cry of preachers, this is the cry of God's people, where are our signs? Where are our miracles? All we're doing is talking about them. Why can't we see 'em?"

His own words condemn him. Not only has he not produced the so-called power that he claims to have seen in the 1950s, but he falsely declared that the 1990s was the final decade. And the viewers respond in droves to his theatrics. He is by far the best weapon TBN has for getting the phones to ring.

During one Praise-a-thon, Paul Crouch was frustrated to see so many phone lines open. "Brother Schambach, come here!" Crouch hollered. "They're not calling! Will you command them to call right now in Jesus' name? Come on, General Schambach!"[173]

Schambach didn't disappoint. There were one hundred phone lines available when Crouch called up Schambach. By the end of his hard-sell plea the available lines lingered around one to three. Schambach appealed to people's greed to give in order to get and they started calling. He ordered the people to pledge $2,000 of what they don't have and to pay the tithe of it ($200) up front. And if they would pay it within ninety days, God would guarantee the rest of the money would come in.

But Schambach put out a warning. "When you get that whole seed," he instructed, "don't you eat your seed. Don't you go down and buy that brand new pair of shoes. Don't buy that new dress. That's seed. You don't eat seed. You put that seed in the ground and then it's gonna spring forth a hundredfold."

Unfortunately for the deceived givers, this was the seventh Praise-a-thon in a row that Schambach gave viewers the revelatory order to give $2,000 in order to get out of debt. At the end of the

Praise-a-thon, he would have a debt-burning ritual. An altar of burning coals was set up outside the TBN studio and Paul Crouch and R. W. Schambach would feed the fire with pledge slips containing the amount of debt the viewers were reporting they wanted rid of. They also included the amount of money there were pledging to TBN to ensure their blessing.

But people were starting to complain that it didn't work for them. No problem, Schambach had a Bible verse to encourage them to give it one more try. He told them the seventh time was the charm as it was for Elijah in 1 Kings 18, who sent his servant out to look for evidence of approaching rain after a long famine.

"You know what?" Paul Crouch said to Schambach. "I had never really thought about that—Elijah and his servant. What if Elijah had quit after that first time? He went and looked and there was no cloud. He went and looked again, again. I had forgotten that. It was the seventh time. What if he had quit the sixth time? There would have been no miracle. There'd have been no rain. There'd have been no story in the Bible, but he hung in there till God heard. I wonder why the Lord waits like that?"

"You know why?" answered Schambach. "For us. I call that prevailing faith, the ability to hang on like a junkyard dog."

But, just in case the old exasperated givers weren't convinced, Schambach looked into the camera and said that he was looking for new partners.

When Schambach first began this campaign during the Fall 1999 Praise-a-thon, he told a testimony of a man who sowed a seed of $500, and the next day he found $25,000 in cash stashed under the hood of his truck, money that did not belong to him.

"Somebody said, 'How did that get there?'" said Schambach. "What are you asking me for? I have an idea some old stingy man trying to hide it from his wife and then he died and nobody knew where it was but the holy ghost." He bought the truck on the same day he found the money, according to Schambach. Obviously he made no attempt to locate the rightful owner, nor did it occur to him to do so. But all's fair in the hundredfold game.

Schambach gave another example of how donors got money to pay their pledges. During the Fall 2000 Praise-a-thon, he shared the testimony of a caller who boasted that the credit card company sent them a check of credit in the amount of $10,000 from which they were able to pay their pledge.

Prosperity pastor Frederick Price, whose program, *Ever Increasing Faith*, airs on many networks, testified of a similarly questionable money strike in the fashion of "finders keepers, losers weepers." In the June 1987 issue of his ministry's newsletter, "Messenger," Price wrote, "Even if you walk down the street and find some money, it still came through some man or woman. It was theirs first."[174]

Once, on a *Behind-the-Scenes* broadcast, Paul Crouch showed a tinge of guilt for the hundredfold hoax. He read a letter that came in from a poor woman in India. Crouch read part of her letter. "At this time I have absolutely nothing," the poor woman wrote, "but I desire to be a source of blessing but also to receive a hundredfold return. I am from India, Bombay. The salary that I get in hand is about 8,400 rupees." Crouch interpreted that to mean about $200 per month salary. She went on, "My husband does not have a job at the moment, therefore a pledge of $2,000, which is what brother Schambach was talking about, is just too much for me. Do I have an option to pledge as much as I can?" she asked. "Dear Jesus, oh," Crouch reacted. "If I let myself, I could weep right now."[175]

Yet, Schambach did not give the poor any such loophole when he commanded the viewers, "If you're down to your last—how many times in my meetings people come and say all I have is $20. I said, you blew it. You should have given it to the Lord. You should have put it in the offering bucket if that's all you have. God begins with nothing."[176]

"I've been doing this at TBN—I'm letting you know what God said," he continued. "I'm not saying this; God told me to rehearse it in the ears of his people. You need a miracle in your life. Anybody can give what they have—but I'm trying to encourage you that have nothing. The meal barrel is empty…there's not enough there but for one more meal. You need a miracle in your bank account…And if you'll be obedient to what the man of God tells you to do, it'll be the beginning of a miracle and it will be perpetual, not just a one-time deal. Obedience is better than sacrifice—that's what the word of God declares."[177]

This sort of spiritual extortion should never be tolerated. Yet TBN can hide behind the First Amendment's freedom of religion clause to legally extort money upon false pretenses. The Crouches don't seem to operate TBN by what's ethical and right, but by what works. As Avanzini once said, blasting ministries who don't teach "give to get" theology, "They can't keep the rent on the building paid, cause what they do don't work."

Schambach made the same accusation against ministries that don't utilize their strong-arm tactics. "Keep it on, heresy hunters. I know you're watching. You can't accuse me of being after your money. You ain't got any!"[178]

PROSPERITY GOSPEL

But what is TBN's gospel? Is it the Gospel of the New Testament? Hardly. TBN's gospel is what is known as the "prosperity gospel." Schambach explained it like this: "When you hear the good news, that God wants you well, you'll not be content to stay in that situation you're in but you'll look for a way out—a way out of your problem; a way out of your trouble and this is why TBN is on—to tell you that we have your answer and the answer is in a person, Jesus of Nazareth."[179]

It is a different gospel, one that is condemned in Galatians 1:6–8:

> I marvel that you are turning away so soon from Him who called you in the grace of Christ, to a different gospel, which is not another; but there are some who trouble you and want to pervert the Gospel of Christ. But even if we, or an angel from heaven, preach any other Gospel to you than what we have preached to you, let him be accursed.

TBN's gospel is under a curse. Money given to TBN is money that is being stolen from the real work of the true Gospel around the world. And TBN makes no bones about taking what they want from the church. "When God speaks to you, you don't have to run to your pastor and say, 'Is it all right? Is it all right for me to give to TBN?'" Schambach told the TBN audience during the Fall 1999 Praise-a-thon. "You ask your pastor and he'll say, 'No, no, you put it right here in the church.' God didn't tell you that! God said to give. You have been feeding twenty-four-hours a day on Christian television and now God wants something out of you. And all He's asking out of you is obedience."

The non-Christians who stumble upon Praise-a-thons see right through the hype. Unfortunately, the true Gospel suffers. One evangelist in Britain put it this way: "In the United States, the prosperity preachers have made 'born-again' a household joke. Born-again is a joke in America because of the prosperity preachers with their money.

When unsaved people see these guys on television, they say, 'This gospel is a con; we don't want your gospel, this is all a con.'"[180]

GAIN BY FALSE TEACHING

One verse the Crouches love to quote out of context is Exodus 34:20. Jan Crouch came up with a twisted interpretation of this passage in 1994 when she told TBN's viewers it says Christians cannot ask God for answered prayer unless they pay money up front. "He depends on us to keep His kingdom going," said Mrs. Crouch. "So we cannot appear before God without a gift."[181]

But, she read the passage from the Living Bible, a paraphrase, not an actual translation, which gives a better rendition for what she was trying to convey. In context, in Exodus 34 God is establishing His requirement for the blood sacrifice for the Feast of Unleavened Bread for the nation of Israel to keep. God could not be approached empty-handed without the blood of the sacrifice. The New Testament teaches that the blood sacrifices in the Old Testament were a shadow of the fulfillment of blood atonement that Christ completed once and for all on Calvary.

Paul Crouch confirmed his wife Jan's distortion of the passage and built upon it to pressure people to pledge support. "We have studied Exodus 34:20; my little sweetheart found this a few years ago," Paul Crouch said to the viewers in a 1998 Praise-a-thon. "You don't stand before God without a gift. The Old Testament, as I've taught you before, you didn't even get into church unless you brought a gift. Hey pastors, what do you think your folks would think if you just stood at the door and said, 'Let me see your tithe before you get in!?' Hello! God did! God did! You didn't get in unless you brought your gift. Hello?! You take it up with God if you don't like this!"[182]

Now this false interpretation has developed into a new TBN doctrine that makes void the blood of Christ and its satisfaction for the sins of believers. They portray God the Father as an angry deity who won't listen to the prayers of His subjects without a bribe.

"You know what? Another thought hit me so strong," Paul Crouch said to "prophet" Mark Chironna during the Spring 2001 Praise-a-thon. "We kind of apologize for tying giving to things that we need from the Lord. Boy, they didn't in the Old Testament. If you had sin in your life, you brought an offering to the priest...If you want God's blessing, He'll make a contract with you...'I'll make a contract. I'll bless you. I'll meet your needs. I'll give you manna from heaven...I'll give you all these things if you'll keep all of my commandments.' And you read them in Exodus 34. The last one is, 'Don't ever come into my house without a gift.' It's just the law of God and the biggest lie the devil has perpetrated on us through the heresy hunters and others is, 'Oh, you can't buy'—We're not buying a miracle of God! We're planting seed in the ground so that a harvest will grow up and give me [wealth]—so that I can establish the covenant, the kingdom of God on this earth. I'm through apologizing for that!"[183]

Wow, Paul Crouch just destroyed the Christian doctrine of the atonement and threw out the New Covenant of the blood of Jesus, our high priest and mediator. The shed blood on Calvary eliminated the need for peace offerings. That's a basic doctrine of the Christian faith.

The Bible warns of a time when apostate Christians will deny Jesus, which is what Crouch does when he looks for another contract. "But there were also false prophets among the people, even as there will be false teachers among you, who will secretly bring in destructive heresies, even denying the Lord who bought them, and bring on themselves swift destruction" (2 Peter 2:1).

I don't know what kind of contract Paul Crouch has made, but the only contract that the New Testament believer is to walk in is the

New Covenant in the blood of the Lamb by which we are saved (and blessed) by grace through faith, not of works lest any man boast. In Crouch's contract, he stands up and boasts continually during the Praise-a-thons of how much money he has given into the work that he fully controls. It's sort of like giving to yourself. Yet with his millions, it's not very impressive when he "sows" $10,000 into a project that furthers his own agenda. That can hardly be seen as giving to God or giving all. He boasts that when he started TBN, they emptied their bank account to do so, but that was not some gift to God, but an investment in his own future. The gamble paid off, but I am not impressed by his so-called generosity. It's what any ambitious businessman would do.

No doubt, it takes a lot of money to keep the network going at its current rate of expansion. The pressure must be great on Paul Crouch to keep the money coming in or else shut down some stations. And if the Seed-Faith heresy pays the bills, it would be self-defeating to recognize its evil and eliminate it. There would be no Crouch dynasty to be passed on to his sons. Paul and Jan Crouch have been snared in this sin trap and cannot break free. The monster must be fed by whatever means it takes. The sin is self-perpetuating in that it leads to more sin just to keep it alive.

As a wise man once said, "The bait you use to catch someone is the food you need to keep them."

"This teaching transferred people's faith in God to faith in our faith," noted the late Martin Lloyd-Jones during the 1960s. "Faith became a force of nature that we could lay hold of and activate to use in our life to live victoriously. The results are the goal, God is not. They lose sight of the fact that we must lose our life to gain it. This is a self-on-the-throne Christianity that is so compatible with the spirit of antichrist."[184]

Crouch has mastered the devilish art of double-speak. He comes right out and says something, then gets angry when he's called on it. He must be getting an awful lot of negative feedback recently since he has begun to defend his false ideas of Seed-Faith giving more and more strongly on every Praise-a-thon. In an agitated voice on April 4, 2001, during the Praise-a-thon, Crouch hollered into the camera:

> If you're sick in body, no you can't buy your healing! No one ever says that! You filthy heretic hunters that try to put that on us. We don't say that! Hear me! We're planting some precious seed in the ground so that a harvest will come up!

Yet, that is exactly the implication of his teaching—that we can't be healed unless we give money first. He doesn't even see the seriousness of what he's saying; he's that deceived. As we'll see more in another chapter, things come out of Crouch's mouth that he isn't even conscious of saying.

GAIN BY FALSE PROPHECY

Up until the new millennium arrived, Paul Crouch continually used the possibility of the Lord returning that year as an incentive for people to give it all while there was still time. In the January 1987 issue of TBN's newsletter, Crouch told his supporters, "Will you go with Jan and me another mile? Will you hold our hands up another year? This could be the final one you know. This could be our 'Battle of the Bulge'!…This final drive will be our finest hour!"

And he reiterated the need to give in the final year of 1990 as well. In the January 1990 newsletter he wrote, "The 1990s will be the last GREAT HARVEST of souls. And YOU and YOUR TBN are a vital part of the HARVEST…This is the time He spoke of when believers would be His witnesses in ALL the World. This is the Final Harvest of Souls before the end comes. The time we have to bring in this last great Harvest is short!"

Benny Hinn was merely following TBN precedent when he announced on the November 9, 1990 Praise-a-thon that there may be only two years before the rapture. Crouch used Hinn's speculation as an incentive to compel the viewers to call in their support: "Dear Lord, this may be the last telethon we'll have to do, maybe the next to the last."

When 1993 rolled around and still no rapture, Crouch put to use another false prophecy to speed up the support. On March 14, 1993, "Reverend" John J. Hinkle of Christ Church in Los Angeles, who buys airtime on TBN, shared a vision allegedly from God with his congregation and the large international TBN audience. "On Thursday night, March the eleventh, the Lord spoke to me in a loud, firm voice," said Hinkle. "'On Thursday, June the ninth, I will rip the evil out of this world.'"

He went on to explain that God was pointing to 1994, not 1993. They would have to wait a year to see the fulfillment. The false prophecy was used by TBN to raise money during their Praise-a-thons and in their newsletter as an incentive for the viewers to give more money than ever before. When June 9, 1993 came and went, no apologies were forthcoming from TBN or John Hinkle.

Apocalyptic sensationalism has proven to be very effective in fleecing the flock. None of the misfires resulted in any apologies by Crouch or Hinn. They just go on to the next false prediction to get the pledges coming in. In the Spring 1999 Praise-a-thon Hinn repeated his dramatics using a false prophecy to extort millions of dollars from unsuspecting victims. He warned TBN's TV audience that 1999 was going to be a year of plenty and the year 2000 would bring disaster.

He threatened the viewers that those who didn't double their giving in 1999 would not survive the year 2000. Even the donors who had already called in their pledges were ordered to call back and increase their giving or face the consequences. This proves Benny Hinn is a false prophet.

This was not the first time Hinn had prophesied falsely. Back in 1989 he prophesied to his congregation at the Orlando Christian Center in Florida what he was seeing for the decade of the 1990s:

- "The Lord also tells me to tell you in mid 90s—about '94 or '95, no later than that—God will destroy the homosexual community of America...He will destroy it with fire."
- "The Spirit of God tells me—an earthquake will hit the East Coast of America and destroy much in the 90s."
- "The Spirit tells me—Fidel Castro will die in the 90s... Holy Spirit just said to me, it'll be worse than any death you can imagine."[185]

After twenty minutes of prophesying to his congregation that night in 1989, Hinn appeared to be "drunk in the spirit." When he came to his senses he said, "I'd like to know what I said. I was totally gone."

Yet no matter how many times Hinn's false prophecies have been exposed, he still performs to overflowing crowds in stadiums around the world.

During the Spring 1999 Praise-a-thon, Paul and Jan Crouch told their viewers that pledges were down because people were nervous about the Y2K scare approaching the new millennium. Hinn exhorted TBN's supporters to not let Y2K fears affect their donations.

Hinn started out by establishing his credentials as a prophet of God. He called upon TBN's fellow guests for help in interpreting a disturbing dream he had had. "I do not fully understand it," he lamented, "but I really believe it deals with what God is about to do in the world."[186]

He gave a long narrative of his mystical dream that he said was "more of a vision of the night" than a dream. "In this dream, I did not see his face," Hinn began. "Everything in me knew it was the prophet Elijah...I walked up to him and he was turning water into blood." Hinn continued, "As I came to him, he said to me, 'Take this!' I took the rod from him."

When he finished, fellow guest Mark Chironna offered the interpretation. "The formless essence of Elijah is the spirit of Elijah that God promised to pour out on the last days' company of seasoned ministry that will literally fulfill everything that God promised under the old covenant that would come into the new covenant of a prophetic order that would change the course of history."

Hinn responded, "I feel the anointing here while he is talking!" Chironna continued, "And when Elijah handed you the rod, God was putting in your hand a new level of apostolic authority for the nations...You are entering into a new age of the miraculous. There will be a sharpening, for the spirit of Elijah rests on you."

Then Hinn laid out his first prophetic message under Elijah's mantle. "Pat Robertson, in January, said, 'I have just come out of two days of prayer and fasting. The Lord has said to me that this year, 1999, would be the greatest year for the body of Christ, economically and spiritually, but beginning the year 2000, disasters would hit in the world, economically and otherwise, and only those in the church who have been giving to God would be spared.'"[187]

Turning his attention to the viewers, Hinn said, "So when I say to you here and in your home, increase your seed, God knows you can and you must because if you do not, you will be the one to suffer."

TBN supporters then jammed the phones in order to survive the coming year of disaster. Hinn gave dire warnings to those that pledge and then fail to follow through: "And one final thing, if you break your promise, hear this! Some of you make a pledge and along the way you decide to forget about it. The Bible says God will destroy the work of your hands if you do that...We can't play games with Him!"

[This is the exact opposite of what R. W. Schambach tells the TBN viewers. He says, "If God doesn't supply it, you don't have to pay it."[188] But he tells the people to go without shoes and clothing and paying creditors, in order to pay TBN's pledge first or the money won't come in for the other things.]

"Now, some of you will have to step out in faith tonight," Hinn said. "You may not even have the money right now. In fact, most times you make a pledge you don't even have it."

Then he followed up with a warning to the skeptics. "You know, you do not get under the kind of anointing I get under just because you sing hallelujah," Hinn said. "There's a heavy price, and I would not want to be in the shoes of the one who touches the anointing. Don't touch the anointing!"

"I'm giving you a prophetic word. You know the scripture says they prospered because they obeyed His prophets. I'm telling you tonight, I'm speaking prophetically. Obey the Lord!"

Hinn had a solution for those who were short on cash—liquidate! "You know if I was you and God spoke to me like this, I'd take it out of my investments to give it to God now 'cause it's already spring and the year 2000 is almost next door."

So now that the year 2000 has come and gone with no casualties to count, will TBN refund the extorted funds? Don't count on it!

THEOLOGICAL PRAGMATISM

Televangelists learn what fads and schemes have worked out for others, and they adapt them for their own financial success. A multiplication of error upon error—false precept upon false precept—has been brought together under TBN's roof. Every trick in the book has been adapted and fine-tuned to get the desired results.

And they ridicule true believers who give with pure motives, calling evil good and good evil. "Like most of you, I was taught that we should give of our resources to God, but NEVER expect anything back from God," wrote Crouch in the March 1999 TBN newsletter. "After all, we should give from a heart of pure love of God simply because He is worthy! Sounds mighty high and noble, doesn't it?" [189]

And the world looks on and laughs. Desperate people look on and empty their pockets because of the power of the Word of God that is being wrongly wielded as a club against them. The words of scripture are powerful, but when wrongly applied they can be devastating. The devil himself recognized that and used God's word taken out of context to tempt Jesus to test God.[190] The devil is the one who inspires others to use the same approach.

TBN's prosperity message is completely foreign to the New Testament teaching on the subject of getting rich off the ministry. The apostle Paul, rather than being a burden to the church, chose to be a tent-maker, along with his partners Priscilla and Aquilla. He told the Corinthians, "Now for the third time I am ready to come to you. And I will not be burdensome to you; for I do not seek yours, but you. For the children ought not to lay up for the parents, but the parents for the children" (2 Cor. 12:14).

Just because there are con men masquerading as brothers does not mean that Christianity is false, as some viewers would conclude.

It just shows that there is so much value in God's kingdom of heaven on earth that opportunists find ways of using it for their own benefit. Jesus gave a parable in which he taught that outsiders would see the value in the community of the saints and try to enrich themselves thereby:

> Then He said, "What is the kingdom of God like? And to what shall I compare it? It is like a mustard seed, which a man took and put in his garden; and it grew and became a large tree, and the birds of the air nested in its branches." (Luke 13:18–19)

The birds of the air are roosting in the branches of God's tree, the true church. The birds live off its fruit and yet are not part of the tree.

Another parable that gives the same imagery is one that TBN regulars admit to often. The Crouches and their guests often boast that they are the violent who take the kingdom by force. They have even hosted "Forceful Men's" conferences based on a misinterpretation of this parable and have identified themselves as the ones who are violent.

"It's time to get violent," R. W. Schambach shouted during the Fall 1999 Praise-a-thon. "The kingdom of heaven suffers violence and the violent take it by force. I'm advocating violence! We've been running from the devil long enough. It's about time we stop in our tracks and turn around and eyeball him and say, 'I've had enough, devil!'"[191]

Schambach was quoting Jesus in the eleventh chapter of Matthew. But it was a rebuke of violent people, not an endorsement of violence. The religious leaders of Jesus' day were using violence against Him so they could have the visible kingdom of heaven for themselves. And today what is known as "the church" has many factions fighting for their position at the top. The same battle for supremacy rages today as it did when Jesus was on earth.

The apostle Peter warned of the same thing as he saw it happening in the first century:

> And through covetousness shall they with feigned words make merchandise of you: whose judgment now of a long time lingereth not. (2 Peter 2:3; KJV)

The prosperity preachers at TBN have turned the Gospel of the Kingdom into the gospel of wealth. These are two different and opposite views. They can't be reconciled. As Jesus said:

> No one can serve two masters; for either he will hate the one and love the other, or else he will be loyal to the one and despise the other. You cannot serve God and mammon. (Matthew 6:24)

"Put on the idiot box if you can bring yourself to watch TBN for any more than ten minutes without getting nauseated," evangelist Jacob Prasch remarked in his message, "Faithful and Unfaithful Bride." "You'll see the Bride of Christ sleeping with Mammon."[192]

Paul Crouch makes it very clear what side of the fence he's on. In his October 1998 TBN newsletter he wrote: "Ah, what a lie the evil one has perpetuated through the scribes and Pharisees of our day! NO! We are not buying this lie anymore! God wants you and me to be RICH in every way!"

It could be that the Crouches began right and got sidetracked. We cannot judge their hearts, but we can and must inspect their fruit. And the fruit of TBN is putrefying. Perhaps the Holy Spirit strove with them for a long time before finally just giving them over to believing the lies they wanted to believe. I hope it's not too late for repentance.

TBN's biggest draw, Benny Hinn, at one time saw through the evil of the prosperity gospel and preached against it. Why did he turn from the truth? God only knows. It's hard to look upon such casualties in the kingdom. Here's some wisdom Hinn once had that he now rejects:

> What's the message out there today? It's a message of ego, pride, and selfishness. It's a message of mine, me, I. Show me how to get more! It's not the message that Jesus preached when He said, "If you want to be my disciples...deny yourself and take up the cross and follow me."[193]

In fact, Hinn was so concerned back in 1987 when he preached this to his congregation at Orlando Christian Center that he said, "Today the Lord has made it very clear to me that I am to warn you today of what's coming. No, this is not an easy message to preach; it is needed. And the Bible tells me if I don't tell you, God will require the blood on my hands!"[194]

"You are as tired and as sick of money-hungry, greedy hypocrites to where you almost threw up," Hinn continued. "They come to empty your pockets, promising you mountains of gold. You haven't gotten one mountain yet!"[195]

And he concluded, "Any preacher that doesn't preach self-denial, the cross, the blood, is a false prophet! Any pastor, any leader, any evangelist that will not preach the cross, the blood, or repentance, living for God, self-denial, is a man filled with ego, selfishness! He's a dreamer!...You say, 'Benny Hinn you're being hard.' No sir! I have seen the heart of God and I want people to see it just like I have seen it...No, this is not a popular message...but it's His [God's] message."[196]

Sadly, only a few years passed before he began proclaiming the same pitiful message. He attributed his change of heart to Oral Roberts. He told the TBN audience during the Spring 1991 Praise-a-thon that Roberts had been a guest at his church in Orlando and criticized Hinn for how he took an offering. Roberts told him, "You take lousy offerings." He told Hinn that he put too much emphasis on giving and little on receiving saying, "From now on build faith in your people, not faith in the seed but faith in the harvest it's gonna bring back." Hinn complied and said, "It changed my whole look on giving and receiving, sowing and reaping."[197]

Later in the Praise-a-thon, Hinn recalled how he used to view mammon. "You know years ago they used to preach, 'Oh, we're gonna walk on streets of gold.' I would say, 'I don't need the gold up there, I got to have it down here.' This is where I need it. I mean it's wonderful to walk on streets of gold in glory, but the bills are down here. Say amen!"

If Hinn had only listened to his own sermon that he preached three years earlier, he might have thrown Oral Roberts out of his church on the spot. At that time, he recognized the evil spirit behind the prosperity gospel and its eventual destruction of souls. Now what he said of them applies to himself. "I fear for these men," said Hinn in that sermon in 1987. "Unless they wake up they may find themselves in a pit they'll not get out of."[198]

CHAPTER EIGHT

LIFESTYLES OF THE RICH AND FAMOUS

The prosperity gospel has evolved over the past fifty years of its existence. Televangelists have adopted various elements of it from each other, customizing its elements to fit their own peculiar vision. There is much debate as to where it all began and who came up with various interpretations of pet verses because of the consistent boasting of the preachers who claim each element as divine revelation given to them directly by God.

One historian points to 1950s faith healer A. A. Allen as an early innovator of mixing faith with prosperity. "Allen was one of the first in the revival to gain support by appealing to the financial dreams of his followers. Implicit in the revival was a conviction that God could grant not only physical but financial healing to His children. Allen early indicated that there was a scriptural secret to financial success."[199]

Apparently, it was during the healing revival movement of the post-war, mid-twentieth century that the Gospel of salvation for man's souls was changed into a false gospel of prosperity. And this at a time when America was beginning to live the American dream of a car in every garage and a television set in every living room. As one teacher put it, "The money preachers—they're simply rewriting the Gospel as a religion of Western consumerism."[200] This was not a movement of God, but a worldly inspiration for a better life and success in the here and now.

Whether or not it was Oral Roberts who came up with the Seed-Faith secret to prosperity, it was Roberts who popularized it and utilized it for his own financial benefit. But it was the preaching of Seed-Faith that worked for Roberts, not the method of sowing and reaping itself. Roberts would preach his new gospel and really lay it on the audience who came to his tent revivals seeking a healing touch from him. At offering time, if you didn't sow money into Roberts' ministry, you weren't about to benefit from his so-called healing virtue.

And because it seemed to work for Roberts, other Pentecostal ministers adopted the concept and put it to work for themselves. Word/Faith heretic Charles Capps said, "Several years ago one of Oral Roberts' books came into my hands, entitled *Miracle of Seed-Faith*. I suppose this book transformed my life as much as any book I have ever read...Oral put it in understandable form so that I could put it to work in my life."[201]

The late Jamie Buckingham, former columnist for *Charisma* magazine and Kathryn Kuhlman biographer, testified that it was Roberts who introduced him to Seed-Faith also. "I remember the afternoon I sat in the audience as Oral spoke. I was still struggling with his 'Seed-Faith' message, and what I felt was an over-emphasis on materialism, but I knew I had to be intellectually honest. That meant letting God flush from my mind all preconceived notions and listening with a clean slate."[202] What that really meant was drowning out the voice of his conscience and the conviction of the Holy Spirit that the Seed-Faith message was indeed carnal and unbiblical.

Role Models for the Crouches

Paul and Jan Crouch continue to this day to uphold Oral Roberts as one of their greatest role models and fathers in the faith. He is still a frequent guest on the *Praise the Lord* program and both Crouches have served on Roberts' ministry boards. It is easy to see from watching TBN and the Crouches' lifestyle how they were impacted by those they honor who led the way in Christian television.

Not only did the Crouches adopt their role models' fundraising methods, but they also followed in their footsteps in living lavishly. When church leaders live in conspicuous consumption, the world looks on and sees right through them. These flock-fleecers rant and rave at the secular press for confronting them on their lavish lifestyles because they justify themselves by saying they are merely enjoying God's promises to bless His children.

Since the Crouches' predecessors seemed to get away with living high on the hog off the donations of the little people, they must have thought they deserved the same benefits. After all, their ministries are bigger than any of their forerunners so they think they deserve the same perks as any CEO of a billion-dollar empire.

PTL & TBN

When the PTL scandal hit the news in 1987, Americans were shocked when their expensive lifestyle was revealed for all to see. Remember the air-conditioned doghouse and the gold plated bathroom fixtures that the secular press made such a big deal out of? Yet today the TBN regulars blatantly flaunt their riches and conspicuous consumption without shame. Few seem to question the impropriety of it nowadays. It's as if it has lost its shock value.

On *Behind the Scenes*, Paul Crouch has often displayed his expensive white Arabian stallion that gets, as has been reported by former staff members, VIP treatment when he makes an appearance and enjoys an air-conditioned portable stable when he is brought to the Irving, Texas studio.

And Paul Crouch's offices in TBN's headquarters in Costa Mesa, California are said to be so luxurious that few people are even allowed onto the third floor of the former Full Gospel Businessmen's Association building where it is located. It has been reported that "Paul Crouch's 8,000-square-foot executive suite, which occupies half of the top floor of the three-story building, is strictly off-limits to the public. Behind doors kept locked throughout construction are a wet bar and sauna, a personal gym, meticulously handcrafted black walnut woodwork and ornate velvet furniture."[203]

The *Orange County Register* reporter who was barred from seeing the suite wrote:

> …but others who have been inside or helped build the suite say it is more befitting a mansion than an office building. "This makes Hearst Castle look like a doghouse," said Steve Oliver, a master journeyman carpenter. While scores of hired hands worked on the exterior and other public areas of the building, Oliver and others in a crew of highly skilled carpenters spent several months last year on Crouch's private third-floor quarters. The finished product is "really rich looking," said Willa Bouwens-Killeen, a Costa Mesa senior planner. "The wood is the very best quality, and they used the best craftsmen," she said. "It looks like something you'd expect in a mansion type of house rather than offices."

The *Los Angeles Times* described the TBN headquarters as "a cross between Disneyland's Sleeping Beauty castle and a Middle Eastern palace. Inside, a sweeping brass and marble staircase leads to a 15-foot tall statue of Michael the Archangel stomping the head of Satan. Behind is a high-definition video theater with a 48-channel sound system and a state-of-the-art television studio."[204]

One Pentecostal preacher who toured the facility was so provoked by what he saw that he produced a video about TBN's decadence entitled, *Temple To The Gods and Goddesses*.[205] In the video Pastor Joseph Chambers shows video clips of his self-guided tour through the areas that are open to the public. As the video scans on the array of red velvet, gold trim, and mirrored walls and ceilings, Chambers gives his commentary:

"Now let's go into the actual headquarters of this temple of the gods and the goddesses," Chambers says while rolling the video footage he took at the newly renovated building. "Watch with me. Nude paintings of cherubim and children all over the ceilings...You'll note that they have female angels, I call them New Age angels, at the entrance along the way as you lead into the studio...Then you have a picture of two nude people hanging over a woman figure...I'm not sure what that picture represents, but it was quite amazing to me. Now if you look, as we take a look around at some other places, there's ancient gods used in decoration. This is on the statues and in different places, the legs of tables. It's all a very motif, a very presence of a temple of the gods and goddesses."[206]

One thing for sure—TBN's décor is done in miserable, poor taste. Many compare the sets and furnishings to ancient brothels. Jan Crouch takes full credit for the interior design. During the Spring 1999 Praise-a-thon, Paul Crouch responded to all the furor that the new studios created. "Oh how the critics rage over a few nice TV studio sets that Jan creates with poly foam and wood columns and a little gold paint! It's all fake folks. It's all fake. It's just a little gilded paint…The heretic hunters just have a field day criticizing Jan and all of us that create a few pretty things that look nice on TV. Of course, God is worthy of it!"[207]

TBN's properties in Hendersonville, Tennessee were formerly owned by country singer Conway Twitty. TBN revamped the stage of the Conway Twitty auditorium to resemble their own Grand Ole Opry with Babylonian trim. The stage is one of the most decadent looking ones in TBN's repertoire, decked out with golden lions on either side of the stage. Jan Crouch told the TBN viewers that she saw the décor in a dream and ordered it to look that way.[208]

So is God worthy of all the fakery and tasteless flamboyance? I guess the décor shows how the Crouches view their God. But Paul Crouch has a point when he compares his temples to Catholic cathedrals. "Hey, if you're gonna get mad, why don't you take the Catholic Church on? I just been over in Italy and I love to go into those beautiful old cathedrals."[209]

Like the late Tammy Faye, Jan Crouch dons tons of make-up and false eyelashes and wigs, sometimes blue or pink-tinted ones. One letter to the editor in *Charisma* magazine said, "I don't judge others by the clothes they wear. However, I can tell you that many people do change the channel because of Jan's extreme appearance. That's unfortunate. Jesus does not want Christians to offend others or cause them to stumble."[210]

The letter was in response to *Charisma's* June 1998 issue that featured TBN as the cover story. In the sidebar, "Jan Will Be Jan," author J. Lee Grady wrote, "Channel surfers who visit the Trinity Broadcasting Network on week-nights often do double takes when they see Jan Crouch chatting on the flashy *Praise the Lord* set. Her pink bouffant wig, heavy eye makeup and constant giggling put her in a category all by herself when it comes to talk-show hosts…She doesn't care if you are offended by her clothing style, her makeup or her recent decision to have cosmetic surgery."[211]

Certainly her appearance does grab the attention of channel-surfers, but diminishes from anything she says since she can't be taken seriously in the minds of the casual viewer.

Tonight Show host Jay Leno once commented on her during his monologue. He said that his wife sometimes watches Christian television and asked his audience if they had seen this woman who "looks like Tammy Faye on a bad day. White hair piled up high, eye make-up that looks like it's applied with a trowel and wearing a fur coat."[212]

Jan Crouch really goes to work during the Christmas holidays. Just like PTL's Heritage USA theme park that lit up every Christmas, TBN's studios come alive in December. Tammy Faye was the first to boast of having one million lights hung on PTL's property, and Jan Crouch has outdone Bakker and has more than one million lights on the Costa Mesa headquarters alone, and perhaps even more all over the newly acquired amusement park they bought in Orlando, the Holy Land Experience.

An article appeared in the December 20, 2000 issue of the *Los Angeles Times* called, "A Glaring Exception: Energy Crisis Puts TBN in an Unfavorable Light." Times staff writer William Lobdell's lead paragraph read, "It's that time of year again: to mail cards, trim the tree—and complain about the light display at Trinity Broadcasting Network headquarters in Costa Mesa. But this December, the complaints—usually centered around matters of taste—have had greater resonance as the state endures its worst energy crisis in more than two decades."

The article went on to explain that TBN made a few concessions to the complaints, but still lit up the building, only for shorter periods of time. The locals in the vicinity say you can see the lights from the TBN building for a mile before you pass by on the 405 Freeway.

One of TBN's brochures boasts of the holiday decorations at their Hendersonville, Tennessee studios. "Marvel at the Yuletide beauty of Christmas City USA. Over a million lights sparkle on 30 acres of beautifully decorated grounds. Stroll through Christmas Around the World and see delightful Christmas traditions from many nations."[213]

Jan Crouch's former personal assistant, Kelly Whitmore, used to have to go and purchase furniture and décor at Crouch's command. "I felt so guilty going and buying those things," said Whitmore. "Christmas lights were absolutely phenomenal in cost."[214]

What a bad portrait of Christianity TBN portrays to the world when they see the gaudy sets and the painted woman that resembles her surroundings. On a *Behind the Scenes* show in December 2000,[215] Jan Crouch gave a guided tour of the conference room at TBNs new Costa Mesa facility. The room was full of banquet tables and chairs and decorated with red velvet curtains. Mrs. Crouch used the time to promote the seminars available to all TBN partners in Southern California. The upcoming seminar was to be conducted by Jan Crouch's own cosmetic surgeon and was on the topic of liposuction.

Paul Crouch also has expensive taste. He once bragged about buying a classic sports car while at the same time claiming that he controls his money, his money doesn't control him. "The Lord gave me a desire of my heart last week," Crouch announced during the Spring 2001 Praise-a-thon. "I got me a little sports car…Yes I did, just like Steve Brock's. He got his a year earlier, yes."[216]

Steve Brock, Benny Hinn's tenor who has also been a regular performer on TBN's *Praise the Lord* programs for a couple of decades, got a good laugh from Crouch's confession.

TBN REGULARS FOLLOW SUIT

The lifestyles of those who have shows on TBN tend to match the example set by the Crouches. There are a few exceptions, but the programming on the network tends to send the same message and give a consistent display of avarice, greed, and worldliness. This is Christianity's biggest embarrassment and shames the name of Jesus Christ, the name that is bantered about on the lips of workers of iniquity.

Recent government investigations into the lifestyles of the top televangelists does not seem to have curtailed much of their conspicuous consumption. It is strange that Paul and Jan Crouch and their sons are not on Senator Grassley's investigation list. Paul Crouch Jr., TBN's chief of staff, called the Senate finance committee's investigation an "inquisition" in an open letter to *Charisma* magazine he wrote in defense of the likes of Kenneth Copeland, Benny Hinn, Creflo Dollar, Joyce Meyer, Paula White, and Bishop Eddie Long. He took issue with *Charisma's* editor Lee Grady's editorial in which he agreed that some accountability was needed in televangelism.

Crouch Jr. put most of the blame on Ole Anthony, head of the Trinity Foundation in Dallas, whom he called a "self-proclaimed reformer of the church." Crouch said that the senator is "playing right into his hands." He added, "We don't need the government to step in and regulate anything when it comes to our faith or the church."

"I don't care if Benny Hinn flies in a private plane, or if Creflo Dollar drives a Bentley," he went on. "That's between them and God. We as Christians are required to give—it's an intrinsic part of our faith. God gave his best to redeem our souls, his only Son, and we are to do the same."[217]

Crouch Jr.'s letter is a sad commentary that he intends to continue in the fleecing of Christianity in the tradition of the dynasty into which he was born. He will pay a large price for gaining the world.

> But now I have written to you not to keep company with anyone named a brother, who is sexually immoral, or covetous, or an idolater, or a reviler, or a drunkard, or an extortioner—not even to eat with such a person. (1 Cor 5:11)

CHAPTER NINE

PROLIFERATION OF FALSE PROPHETS

Christian television networks give modern-day false prophets and false teachers a platform from which to internationally fleece the flock of God. Not only are Christians fleeced of their money, but even worse, they are fleeced of their faith. Many believers are shipwrecked in their faith when Christian leaders they have trusted are discovered to be wolves in sheep's clothing. Those who are not grounded in the Word of God throw all of Christianity out the window when their favorite teachers are revealed to be religious con men.

It is a serious matter when Jesus is discredited around the world because of those misrepresenting Him. Paul rebuked the hypocrites of his day saying,

For the name of God is blasphemed among the Gentiles because of you. (Romans 2:24)

We are warned throughout the Bible that in the latter days deceivers would rise up among us leading many astray. This sign is being fulfilled today, and networks like TBN and GodTV are at the forefront of spreading this apostasy. Jesus warned that false christs and false prophets would proliferate just before His return (see Matthew 24) and it is one of the signs prophesied to increase as the Day of the Lord approaches. Ultimately, the man whom the Bible calls "the second beast" or "the false prophet" will come on the scene and deceive the world into following after the first beast—the antichrist.

The apostle Peter warned that false prophets would rise up among us, not in the cults outside the church walls—evangelical Christians can see through Mormons and Jehovah's Witnesses and Moonies. Peter tells us three times in his epistles, "Be sober in spirit," yet today people are getting drunk in the spirit and boast that it's from God.

Jesus did not say that men would come in the name of Jesus, but in the name of Christ, claiming to be him. Another term for "Christ" is "the anointed one." Jesus Christ is the only "anointed one" in the true New Testament sense. However, on Christian television today many preachers claim to be "God's anointed." "Touch not God's anointed" is another way of telling people not to test or question anything they say or do.

Eventually when the antichrist arrives on the scene, he will try to convince the world that he is the long awaited Messiah. Jesus warned of this when he told the Jewish leaders, "I have come in my Father's name and you will not receive me. A time is coming when another will come in his own name and him you will receive" (John 5:43).

The Bible depicts the antichrist as one who will deceive the world with lying signs and wonders. He will attempt to duplicate the miracles that marked the life of Jesus and will mislead many. Satan's strategy was previewed in a book that caused a stir back in 1965. It was called *The Passover Plot*. Author Dr. Hugh Schonfield argued that the historical Jesus tried to replicate Old Testament prophecies of a coming Messiah in order to deceive the Jews into believing he was their deliverer.

The Passover Plot impressed Bible scoffers who were looking for anything to justify themselves in their own agnosticism. Schonfield begins his thesis like this:

> It is the moment before sundown in Jerusalem. On the hill of Golgotha three bodies are suspended on crosses. Two, the thieves, are dead. The third appears so. This is the drugged body of Jesus of Nazareth, the man who planned his own crucifixion, who contrived to be given a soporific potion to put him into a deathlike trance. Now Joseph of Arimathea, bearing clean linen and spices, approaches and recovers the still form of Jesus. All seems to be proceeding to plan.[218]

As *The Passover Plot* accuses the real Christ of tampering with evidence and staging events to look like prophetic fulfillment, the antichrist will be the one to use such deception to get people to believe in him.

One Old Testament prophecy the antichrist will have to counterfeit is the ministry of Elijah who is prophesied to precede the Second Coming of Christ. John the Baptist was the forerunner for Jesus at His first coming, and the Lord promised that before His return, Elijah indeed will come. So it follows that the false prophet will prepare the way for the antichrist to arrive on the scene by counterfeiting the ministry of John the Baptist.

As the time of the Lord's return nears, the actual false prophet will have to be busy at work in advance of the unveiling of the antichrist. The religious side of this demonic duo would be the first to show up on the scene. There have been many speculations about who could be the antichrist, but few pondered the man who comes before. Many potential antichrists have come and gone throughout history along with a plethora of many false prophets.

Bible prophecy gives clues to the attributes of the ultimate false prophet:

- He will be male;
- He will need a mode of communication to the whole world (Christian satellite networks, perhaps?);
- He will be sought after by kings and secular leaders;
- He will be money-hungry—he can be bought;
- He will be charismatic in the charming sense of the term;
- He will be ecumenical;
- He will have diabolical power;
- He will be recognized by all minor false prophets;
- He will fulfill false prophecies made by false predecessors;
- He will claim Elijah's mantle;
- He will seem to walk in the supernatural;
- He will devalue Jesus Christ and elevate mankind;
- He will give false prophecies;
- He will corrupt the uniqueness of Jesus Christ, God the Son.

Over the past two thousand years there have been instances of people claiming to be prophets, such as Nostradamos. In the past they have always been written off as kooks by the church at large. Even in the Dark Ages when so-called holy men beguiled many, they did not refer to themselves as prophets, but mystics. It has only been in the last hundred years that the idea that God was restoring prophets and apostles to the church has gained wide acceptance with the aid of Christian television and more recently the Internet.

Leading up to the time this lesser beast takes center stage, the god of this age[219] raises up false prophets with extra-biblical revelation who make predictions that the devil intends to bring to fulfillment.

Part of that revelation is a distortion of end-times prophecy. The Bible presents a picture of the church of the last days going into great apostasy with only a remnant holding onto the truth. The new "prophets" present a victorious united church that will take dominion over the earth so that Jesus can return.

One popular book that came out in the late 1980s called *Held in the Heavens Until* popularized the false teaching that says that Jesus cannot return until the church takes full dominion of the earth. It was written by the late Earl Paulk, a former mega-church pastor in Atlanta who died under a dark cloud after several women in his congregation sued him for sexual misconduct.

Paulk adopted his teaching from latter rain/manifest sons[220] teachers who came before him. Paulk reasoned that since all things will be put under Jesus' feet[221] and the church is the body of Christ, then since the feet are in the body, the church must put all things under its feet.

Paulk taught that Jesus is waiting for the formation of an unblemished bride to be perfect in holiness and ruling the earth before He can return. According to Paulk, the Second Coming of Christ "will only come when that which is perfect, which is God's kingdom revealed among us in perfection in such degree that you have a...church that is so following God that perfection walks on the earth just like Jesus did."[222]

This "manifest sons" doctrine was introduced by William Branham in the 1940s and denounced by the Assembly of God denomination. It denigrates the Lord Jesus and has an unbiblical view that the church will become a new breed of believers that will overcome sickness and even death before the resurrection of the saints.

The only place in the Bible that it can be found that men can overcome death with their feet planted on the ground is in the book of Revelation. "In those days men will seek death and will not find it; they will desire to die, and death will flee from them" (Rev. 9:6).

Paulk debated his dominion theology with Bible prophecy teacher Hal Lindsey on TBN; that was the last time Paul Crouch would allow any doctrines to be debated on his network. After the Paulk/Lindsey debate, Crouch wrote to TBN supporters in the October 1987 newsletter,[223] "First of all—JESUS IS COMING AGAIN! On that we all agree. The danger here as we examine the truths of the Kingdom is that satan is trying to use the honest and sincere pursuit of truth as a divisive wedge to cause this mighty army of God to break rank, cease our spiritual warfare and dissipate all of our spiritual energies wrangling and disputing over non-essential matters while the world pursues its headlong plunge toward Hell! I speak by the word of the Lord that THIS SHALL NOT BE! I now agree with you that this fiendish tactic of satan is now BOUND IN THE NAME OF JESUS! AMEN" (emphasis in original).

Crouch made it quite clear whose side he chose—that of the obvious false prophet Paulk. Crouch continued, "Oh beloved Partners, don't you see it? Jesus won the Victory. He handed the title deed of this world back to us, His Body! But it is one thing to have legal title to a property and quite another matter to have actual possession of it!…Today, Glory be to God, satan is no longer the undisputed Prince of the Power of the Air! We are pulling his strongholds down now and ESTABLISHING THE KINGDOM OF GOD in the airwaves! GLORY!…We are possessing the Kingdom!"[224]

Since that time TBN's vision began to change from an expectancy of the Lord's soon return into a pursuit of power and domination over the airwaves. The emphasis on money for expansion took an evolutionary leap—mostly thanks to an immoral man in Atlanta who lost a debate but won the day for an earthly kingdom.

KANSAS CITY FALSE PROPHETS

When a prophet speaks in the name of the Lord, if the thing does not happen or come to pass, that is the thing which the Lord has not spoken; the prophet has spoken it presumptuously; you shall not be afraid of him. (Dt. 18:22)

The Bible established the criteria of God's prophets at 100 percent accuracy. That criteria needed to be altered to prepare the way for modern-day prophets to have a prominent place in church leadership.

Rick Joyner, on his *MorningStar* television program aired on Sky Angel justified his prophetic misfires by saying, "There is a freedom to do wrong. There's the freedom to misrepresent him [Jesus] and make many mistakes which Christians have done from the very beginning...But you know that was all OK with God, we're like his children. He knows we're trying." [225]

But is it okay to make false prophecies, claiming that God spoke when He didn't? It's one thing to say, "I think this might happen..." and quite another to say, "The Lord spoke to me and said..." What does God really think about it? Here's what the God of the Bible tells us to do about those who prophesy falsely:

Thus saith the LORD of hosts, Hearken not unto the words of the prophets that prophesy unto you: they make you vain: they speak a vision of their own heart, and not out of the mouth of the LORD. (Jer. 23:16; KJV)

That is certainly a good strategy for any Christian living in these perilous times. If any teacher speaks falsely, claiming to have received his words directly from God, the Bible says not to listen to them. They are not to be trusted with anything of a spiritual nature after doing that; they have lost all credibility. These are people who add to and take away from the Word of God.[226]

Joyner was not the first one to popularize the notion that prophets have the freedom to prophesy falsely in God's name. He rose to prominence in an incarnation of the latter rain movement in the 1980s known as the Kansas City Prophets. Under the banner of Grace Ministries, headed by Mike Bickle, these prophets such as Paul Cain, Bob Jones, Jack Deere, and John Paul Jones wreaked havoc in the church. John Wimber, the then head of the Vineyard Christian Fellowships, stepped in to supposedly bring some accountability and pastoral guidance. Wimber is best known as a leader in the charismatic movement who broke from Calvary Chapel in the 1970s over differences regarding spiritual experience. His "Signs and Wonders" class at Fuller Theological Seminary was controversial in that he taught his students how to "do the stuff" of the gifts as if the gifts of the Spirit could be learned.

Wimber promoted the idea that modern prophets can make mistakes in the name of the Lord and still be considered valid prophets. "Prophet" Bob Jones (not to be confused with the namesake of Bob Jones University) was found to have used his "ministry office of prophet" to get women to disrobe in front of him by the Lord's command. To this day leaders in the apostolic/prophetic movement still look to Jones as an anointed prophet in spite of his moral failures.

Wimber's involvement was sparked by a 233-page report that was widely circulated by Ernie Gruen, a pastor in Shawnee, Kansas who, because of his proximity to Kansas City, compiled various complaints about the "prophets" from their victims. Included in the report were testimonies from those whose lives were hurt by these "immature prophets." The report[227] summarized Grace Ministries' concepts of prophecy and prophets. Its list included:

- "Have experiences which indicate they have been sovereignly chosen by God (miraculous birth, angelic visitations, etc.)."
- "Receive constant flow of revelatory information—'more at home in heaven than on earth.'"
- "Almost a constant flow of divine revelation."
- "Many 'open visions' ('I was there…')."
- "New Testament prophecy is a mixture and inaccurate." (Mixture of accurate and inaccurate words)
- "They call people prophets because they have had supernatural visitations."
- "They call people prophets because they have the audacity to give weird, off-the-wall prophecies concerning future events in the nation and world."
- "They give personal predictive prophecies that do not come true."
- "They excuse error by saying they are immature and in the process of seeing prophets restored."
- "Under the New Covenant, prophets make mistakes and are inferior to Old Covenant prophets."

The late John Wimber defended Grace Ministries but eventually disassociated himself without so much as an apology for misleading so many. In fact, the repercussions of Wimber's redefinition of a prophet is felt today with a plethora of Christianized psychics masquerading as prophets without the biblical requirement of 100 percent accuracy. Wimber's official position on behalf of the entire charismatic movement was that prophets need not be tested to be true or false based upon their accuracy or lack thereof.

In an article in Vineyard's magazine, *Equipping the Saints*, called "Introducing Prophetic Ministry," Wimber wrote, "Babies are messy and they make messes. Their messes must be cleaned up regularly. One minute they need a spanking, the next they need a loving touch...If babies grow in obedience and trust, they soon make fewer messes and require less attention...Eventually baby prophets become contributing members of the family. I suspect that's how prophetic ministries will develop in the Vineyard."[228]

Wimber validated other false moves of the unclean spirit that blew through the church from the beginning of his "ministry" right through to the end. He gave his full support to the Toronto Airport Christian Fellowship pastored by John Arnott until the supposed revival degenerated into manifestations that were unseemly. It was reported to Wimber that young people at the Airport Vineyard were clucking like chickens and barking like dogs during the holy laughter services. Wimber gave Arnott an ultimatum to curtail the animal noises and to calm the chaos or leave the umbrella of the Vineyard. Arnott chose to sever the relationship and Wimber moved on without so much as an apology to all those who were deceived by Arnott due to Wimber's hasty backing.

The end came November 17, 1997, when Wimber died of a massive brain hemorrhage after suffering for several years with cancer of the sinuses. An emaciated John Wimber had appeared on the January 25, 1994 *Praise the Lord* program and told hosts Paul and Jan Crouch how he contracted cancer. He traced it to an evangelistic meeting in which he spoke in the city of Hong Kong a year before. He said, "I had over three thousand people saved in one altar call. It was and is the highlight of my ministry life."[229]

"I got the impression from the Lord that this was going to be contested," he continued. "Well, I don't know for sure, but I think that I got a Chinese cancer that night from a demon…Later on, a demon spoke to me audibly, in my head, but I heard it as an audible voice, about 'I'm going to kill you.'"

Wimber confessed that he was afraid of death and that just before this incident he had gotten a letter from an unnamed minister who rebuked him for his false teachings. Wimber said, "He was writing me this letter saying that because you've done thus and so, God's going to take your life." He said that his wife took the letter and stood upon "2 Kings 9:14 just as Hezekiah took his letter in…she prayed it through." The hate mail may have been spurred by Wimber's involvement at that time with the popular holy laughter movement in Toronto that he initially endorsed only to later disassociate himself.

As it turns out, the answer to his wife's prayer was "no." During the interview Wimber kept spraying something into his mouth. He could no longer produce his own saliva because of a loss of salivary glands caused by his condition. He commented, "One of my six-year-old grandchildren was asking me the other day, 'What is that, Grandpa?' And I said, 'Well, it's spit.' 'Well, where did you get it?' And I said, 'From pigs,' and he said, 'Grandpa, that's gross!'"

What a sad ending to the life of the man who brought credibility to the new false prophets that eventually leavened much of professing Christianity and most certainly influenced the Crouches and other leaders in Christian television.

PROPHETIC INACCURACY

Arnott protégés Wes and Stacey Campbell reinforced Wimber's and the Kansas City Prophets' redefinition of the gift of prophecy as hit or miss. Wes Campbell compared New Testament prophets to oxen in a stall. He said they leave messes and one has to sift through all their manure in order to find a nugget hidden within it.[230]

His wife Stacey made a similar observation about "the prophetic." She said, "It could be out and out wrong. Nobody's perfect. Everybody gets some wrong sometimes. They can get nine out of ten, nine out of a hundred, but they're gonna get one wrong...Judge it and see for yourself and it's a fifty-fifty split."[231]

That was her conclusion after giving an illustration of prophetic accuracy by saying, "When I look into my behind, I see that it is divided into two equal parts. And I kind of see prophecy that way, that it is divided into two equal parts."

Bible teacher Jacob Prasch, after viewing this clip of the Campbells, had this reaction: "You know in witchcraft you have this mixture of a percentage right and a percentage wrong. What is the difference between Wes and Stacey Campbell and witchcraft unless the standard of the Word of God is upheld?"[232]

Wes Campbell did not originate the idea of prophecy being like the ox in a stable. It came from Grace Ministries' Mike Bickle, who penned it in a special prophetic edition of his newspaper, the *Grace City Report* in the Fall 1989. Both men used Proverbs 14:4 for their inspiration. It reads: "Where no oxen are, the manger is clean, but much increase comes by the strength of the ox." Bickle interprets that passage as an encouragement "to be patient with sincere ministries, though they might be immature, because they will bear more fruit in due season as they grow up. If we kill them off with criticism and impatience before they flower, then we have gained nothing."[233]

This idea that a prophet gets more accurate as he practices his craft is downright occultic. Though percentages may be true for psychics, it is never the case in the Bible for true prophets. One writer noted, "God used a well-known prophet as a child—Samuel with Eli—with no 'developing' of his prophetic 'skills.' There is no indication at all in the Scripture that 'young prophets' are less 'accurate' than 'more developed' prophets. God is the same today, yesterday, and tomorrow. The gifts He gives are as timeless and 'mature' as He is. We have never known it otherwise."[234]

Paul Crouch welcomed KC prophet, Paul Cain onto the set of TBN's *Praise the Lord* in March of 1994, believing Cain's credentials to be valid. "I have wanted Paul Cain to come for a long time," Crouch said. "A brother who moves in the office of the prophet… Brother Paul Cain, prophet of the Lord, welcome to *Praise the Lord* tonight! I picked up a book the other day that mentioned you and some of the things that you have seen in the spirit; and it wasn't actually from a supporter of yours. It was from one of the heresy hunters, but that kind of got me interested and it was one of the reasons why I invited you to come."[235]

One of Cain's major false prophecies is that a new breed of prophet would arise before the Lord's return that he referred to as "Joel's Army." This seemed to be a rehash of the vision of the latter rain/manifest sons outpouring that was first promoted by the late heretic William Branham. As a young man in the late 1940s Cain had participated in some of Branham's crusades. "William Branham [was] the greatest prophet that ever lived, in any of my generation, or any of the generations' revival that I've lived through," Cain was quoted as proclaiming in a taped message called "Joel's Army."[236] (The new "prophets" misinterpret the second chapter of the book of Joel as being a last days army of overcomers when in fact it is a demonic army that is described in Revelation 9.)

Many of today's prophets, including Paul Cain and Benny Hinn, have glorified Branham in spite of the fact that he is a proven false prophet who taught that the new millennium and the return of Christ would happen in 1977. However, he did not live to see this non-event because he died in an auto accident in 1965. His followers expected him to rise from the dead and delayed his burial waiting for him to come back to life.

The late Lester Sumrall often spoke of this expected outpouring before the Lord's return as he heard it from one of Branham's contemporaries, Smith Wigglesworth. Sumrall said that a dying Wigglesworth told him, "The dead will be raised...cancer will be healed...no disease would be able to stand before God's people and that it would be a world-wide situation—not local...thrust of God's power and anointing upon mankind...I will not see it but you shall see it."[237]

Yet Sumrall died in 1996 and nothing even close to what was described happened before his death.

LIKE FATHER, LIKE SON

Oral Roberts, a contemporary of Branham and Wigglesworth, is honored by the Crouches and many of today's new prophets as a pioneer in the prophetic movement, even though his record of hearing from the Lord is abysmal. As noted earlier, the Crouches have Roberts to thank for giving them the key to the viewer's wallets—the Seed-Faith heresy. Christian media expert Al Dager, of Media Spotlight, gave the following summary of Oral Roberts' ability to hear accurately from the Lord:[238]

- 1960: Roberts claimed that God had told him to make His healing power known throughout the earth.
- 1977: Roberts said he had received a vision from God telling him to build the City of Faith. He later claimed to have seen a nine-hundred-foot-tall Jesus who told him that the vision would soon be realized and that the hospital would be a success. The City of Faith opened in 1981.

- 1983: Roberts announced that Jesus had appeared to him in person and commissioned him to find a cure for cancer (*Time*, July 4, 1983).
- 1986: Roberts said God had told him, "I want you to use the ORU medical school to put my medical presence in the earth. I want you to get this going in one year or I will call you home. It will cost $8 million and I want you to believe you can raise it" (*Abundant Life*, Jan/Feb. 1987).
- January 1987: Roberts said God had told him…he had to raise $8 million by March 1 or God would take him home. Roberts said the money would be used to provide full scholarships for medical missionaries who would be sent to Third World countries…He said $3.5 million had been raised and all he needed was $4.5 million before March 1 that year.
- April 1, 1987: Roberts announced that he had raised $9.1 million—$1.1 million more than needed. Of the money raised, $1.3 million was given by a dog track owner, Jerry Collins.
- November 1987: Roberts announced that the City of Faith medical clinic will close in three months.
- January 1988: Roberts canceled the university's free medical tuition program despite his claim that God had told him to make the medical school a world outreach program.
- March 1988: The medical scholarship fund went bankrupt. Students were required to repay scholarship funds at 18 percent annual interest if they transferred to another school rather than stay at ORU medical school and start paying the high tuition.
- September 1989: Roberts decided to close the medical school and the City of Faith hospital to pay off debts.

"When Oral Roberts says that God told him that he was going to take him home if he didn't get 8 million dollars, he lied to the public," noted the original Bible Answer-man Walter Martin. "God never told him that at all. Don't you get the feeling that something's going wrong? It is and it's found for you in scripture. We're told in scripture to reprove, rebuke, and exhort...for the time will come when men will not put up with sound doctrine...It's here."[239]

Author Dave Hunt also summed up Oral Roberts' record for hearing from God:

How about Oral Roberts? You know he had a seven-hour conversation with a nine-hundred-foot Jesus who told him to build a hospital in Tulsa that anybody knew wasn't needed. Promises that there will be miracles, a cure for cancer, 777 beds. You know three sevens—that's terrific! I don't think they ever had more than 246 of them occupied. The thing went bankrupt. No cure for cancer. No miracles. Is that a false prophecy? You have to ask yourself seriously. Was Oral Roberts just lying to us or was he hallucinating or did he really have this conversation? I mean a seven-hour hallucination? That's pretty long. Did he really have a conversation with some nine-hundred-foot being that claimed to be Jesus? That's quite a delusion! But he continues to be quite popular.[240]

Oral's son Richard Roberts followed in his father's footsteps. He just stepped down as the president of Oral Roberts University in Tulsa amidst allegations of misappropriation of funds and other charges leveled against him and his current wife Lindsay by three ORU professors.

On Richard and Lindsay Roberts' show, *Something Good Tonight*, that aired in March 2000, Richard Roberts told the ORU students in the chapel service that God spoke to him in an audible voice and said, "'I want you to get my university out of debt.' Students, I prophesy and I'm not a man that prophesies very often unless God gives me a word. I prophesy to you...I prophesy that we are very near to the day when this university is going to be totally debt-free...Every one of you who are sowing seed...Students, if you've not been sowing seed you don't have a right to this prayer. God is not going to multiply what you don't sow. But if you have been sowing seed then I want you to lay your hands on my hands...we're going to break the spirit of debt off of you who are giving."

Of course, none of these students were part of the now defunct medical program at ORU, but were liberal arts students, many of whom gave up their spending money so that the Roberts family could get ORU out of its reported 33 million dollar debt.[241] Richard Roberts often bragged, "When you see me, you've seen my father." False prophesying worked for his father, so no doubt the younger Roberts deduced it would work for him as well. The biggest losers in the deal were those struggling ORU students.

Paul Crouch's son Matthew and his attractive wife Laurie are regular hosts of *Praise the Lord*. They often invite guests onto the program that claim the title of prophet or apostle. Matt Crouch presented his view on the subject of modern-day prophets on a *Behind-the-Scenes* program in October of 2002. "We're starting to see prophets go to the White House," he said. "Mark Chironna went to the White House after declaring a prophetic word over the White House. Kim Clement went to the White House...It's the time of the prophet!...I believe this is a prophetic generation."[242]

PSYCHIC PROPHETS

Mark Chironna is a regular on TBN who frequently hosts *Praise the Lord* and the Praise-a-thons. He declared Benny Hinn to be the fulfillment of the coming of Elijah and in return, Hinn recognized Chironna as a true prophet. Chironna, like Kim Clement, has mastered what is known in the Psychic Network as "cold readings," convincing Christians they are practicing the gift of personal prophecy.

Chironna, like so many others, points to the coming times of power and dominion, known as the latter rain, that the Crouches have embraced as a call to TBN. He introduced the TBN audience to super-prophet Bill Hamon, a writer of the latter rain/manifest sons heresy and author of the 1987 book *Prophets and Personal Prophecy: God's Prophetic Voice Today*. Chironna told Hamon that his book, *The Eternal Church* had a profound impact on his own ministry and that he read the book so many times that he had to hold it together with a rubber band.[243]

Hamon conducts Schools of the Prophets and teaches people how to prophesy, as if the gifts of God can be learned. He claims to have a gift of impartation to lay hands on people and impart on them the gift of prophecy. When Hamon was a guest on the *Saints Arise* program seen on Sky Angel, he told host Gary Greenwald how he activates somebody to prophesy. He begins by asking the charismatic believer, "'Do you pray in other tongues?' And they'll say, 'yes.' I say, 'Well, do you make the Holy Ghost talk when he doesn't want to? What if he's not in the mood to talk?'...So I tell them if you tell me how you can pray in tongues, I can tell you how I prophesy. We both do it by faith and the grace of God and faith in operating in that gift of God, that's already in us."[244]

This is the same rationalization "holy ghost bartender" Rodney Howard-Browne used to initiate his audiences into holy laughter.

Just start doing by faith—in your own power—and then the holy ghost will take over. One error builds upon an earlier error. In the 1960s Episcopal bishop Dennis Bennett, a leader in the charismatic renewal, taught this do-it-yourself method to learning how to speak in other tongues—do it by faith.[245]

Most of the lesser prophets point to Benny Hinn as the one with the greatest anointing of all. He is certainly the most respected. But he has lots of competition from other prophets vying for the title of the forerunner of Christ. The Lord's warning in Matthew 24 of the rise of false prophets is being fulfilled in our day and Christian television is the medium of choice.

CHAPTER TEN

THE FORERUNNER MINISTRY

These are called lying signs and wonders. Brother, there is such a thing as signs and wonders produced by a lie—people getting healed, people falling under the power because of a lie, not because of truth. I'm telling ya, I've really had to ask the Lord if I should be teaching this tonight because I am fed up with it. I am seeing enough on Christian television even, that I'm fed up with. Just because it's Christian TV, it doesn't mean it's God. May I say it again, just because it's aired on Christian television, it does not mean it's God. I'm sorry to be so blunt, I think sometimes they air those things to get an offering. I'm sick and tired of it. Quit using the airwaves with a lie to raise money! Enough of it.[246]

Words of wisdom from Mr. Flamboyant himself, Benny Hinn, speaking at the 2008 Fire Conference in Louisville, Kentucky. Sort of like the pot calling the kettle black. Without naming names, he identified what had gotten his ire up:

There was a so-called revival recently in Florida that was not a true revival. That was not a move of God and thousands of people flew from all over the world believing God is in it. And I'm glad, thank God for the Assemblies of God who stood against it. And it's not a real move. Somebody had to

say something about it. Now precious people, I think it's
about time you understand not every evangelist is a true
servant of God and not everyone who mentions the name
"Jesus" is a servant of God. Signs and wonders happen in
the demonic realm also. Just because people fall under the
power, it doesn't mean it's God.[247]

He could only be referring to the tattooed evangelist, Todd Bentley, who had made a big splash in Lakeland, Florida earlier that year,
2008, only to end in a scandal when he left his wife and children
for another woman, whom he quickly married when the divorce
was final. All the antics were carried on GodTV and promoted as
the latter rain outpouring by such luminaries as Bob Jones, former
Kansas City prophet whose own reputation was tainted several years
ago when it was discovered that he used his bogus office of prophet
to get women to disrobe for him. Now Rick Joyner of MorningStar
Ministries in North Carolina is taking Bentley under his wing to
restore him to profitable ministry, sanctifying his adulterous marriage to a younger woman.

GodTV's co-founder, Wendy Alec, had been given a supposed
word from the Lord to give her full support to this "revival" that
rose up through the same family as the Toronto outpouring a decade
earlier. The Bentley outpouring began at Ignited Church, pastored
by Stephen Strader, the son of Karl Strader whose Carpenters Home
Church in Orlando was the birthplace of the holy laughter craze of
Rodney Howard-Browne.

Hinn rightly discerned the unholy nature of the Bentley revival,
but fully endorsed Toronto. Perhaps if he knew that the holy laughter craze got to Toronto via a man laughing at someone imitating a
pig he might have thought twice.

New Wine, a pro-Toronto resource on the Web, published a

history of the *Toronto River Revival* that traces the spiritual manifestations at John Arnott's church back to Howard-Browne via former Vineyard pastor Randy Clark.

Clark shared at the "Catch the Fire" conference in Toronto on October 13, 1994 that after a period of spiritual dryness in 1993 he was close to a breakdown. A friend invited him out to a meeting at Kenneth Hagin's Rhema Bible Church in Tulsa where Howard-Browne was the featured guest. Clark was hesitant since he did not care for the Word/Faith, name-it-and-claim-it crowd, but the Lord supposedly spoke to him about his "denominational spirit," so he went along.

When he arrived he was taken aback by a woman laughing hysterically and thought to himself that she was in the flesh. "At the third meeting that they attended," the New Wine article reported, "Randy fell under the power when Rodney prayed for him…in 1989 at the Vineyard, he had been filled, but with shaking. But this time, there was no shaking, and this caused Randy to doubt that the experience was real. He thought, 'I'm weak minded. I'm just falling under suggestion.' But when he tried to get up, he found that he was unable to do so. It was as though he was pinned to the floor. He had been in a line of people who had been filled, and 'two bodies down from me, there was somebody oinking.' This caused Randy to start laughing, and he couldn't stop. After he finally got up, he got more and more drunk in the Spirit."[248]

When Clark returned to his own Vineyard church in St. Louis, everyone he laid hands upon now received the laughter bug. When John Arnott, pastor of the Toronto Airport Vineyard heard about the outpouring, he invited Clark in to "introduce the prophetic." That began the Toronto revival that denigrated into chaos in the name of Christ.

Toronto Airport Vineyard was renamed TACF, Toronto Airport

Christian Fellowship, after Wimber asked Arnott to step down from the Vineyard. It has spawned an even darker deterioration of Christianity and is associated with an umbrella group called "The Elijah List" that consists of new so-called prophets who specialize in chaotic signs and wonders.

Benny Hinn is not recognized as one of Elijah List's prophets, though TBN regular Kim Clement is. Could it be professional jealousy that triggered Hinn's declaration of war against the List's associates such as Todd Bentley? After all, it was Hinn who first popularized the calling down of "fire" upon his followers that set the stage for the metaphysical game played at TACF called "fire tunnels," where young people form a two-row line and scream "fire" at the power-seekers as they walk down the middle.

"Prophet" Mark Chironna declared Hinn to be the coming of the forerunner, Elijah, in fulfillment of Jesus' prophecy that Elijah would come before His return. Oral Roberts confirmed Chironna's proclamation and conferred upon Hinn his own spiritual mantle. "Elijah List" on the other hand, claims a corporate fulfillment of the Elijah mantle upon their own company of prophets! All modern-day false prophets are vying for Elijah's identity.

Hinn exhorted his Kentucky audience to test all manifestations seen on Christian television since they could be from the demonic realm. He said:

> If I ever stood on a platform and said, "I have been to heaven and seen Jesus," leave my meeting. If I have ever said that angels talk to me on a daily basis, leave the service. If I ever tell you that I have known the name of angels in glory, leave the service. If I ever tell you I can take you to heaven with me to visit Jesus, leave the service. Yet some—please for-

give me—simple-minded people have sat in meetings and listened to such nonsense of people telling them they have visited heaven and gone and talked to Abraham and had coffee with him. Where is it in the Bible?[249]

BENNY HINN UNDER THE MICROSCOPE

Using the above criteria, can Benny Hinn's own ministry over the years bear up under such scrutiny?

Over his career, Hinn has startled many viewers of his daily program, *This is Your Day* and TBN's *Praise the Lord* with his guttural anointing and stories of both friendly and hostile spirit visitors. Even his own children are frightened when he takes on a different persona or as Hinn puts it: "When the anointing hits me I change; Benny becomes a different boy, and something happens inside of me."[250] "I do not even identify with the Benny Hinn you see on television because it's a different man; it's not me. My children are afraid of me under the anointing. What they do not know is that I'm afraid of the anointing too."[251]

Hinn afflicted his own children with this power: "When God touches your children in your meeting it's special! And my little Joshua who wouldn't have known a thing about what's been going on in our meetings, when the power of God hit him—now he's only eight years old—he began to vibrate. You saw him! And you saw him! It was awesome! I never expected to see my kid do the same things all the other kids were doing…I'm telling you it's real. When it hits your kid, it's real!"[252]

Was it really the power of God that "hit" that child, vibrating uncontrollably with a confused and startled look on his face? During another of his meetings where this so-called "electrical current" hit the people, his niece came to the platform displaying this diabolical manifestation. She jerked and shook along with many other youth whose trembling bodies covered the entire platform.

A couple of weeks after this meeting in Denver, Colorado, Hinn commented on it on a *Praise the Lord* program. "I've not seen the power of God I'm seeing now in our meetings...I mean to see the kids electrocuted...Three people had that experience that were thrown, and I'm not sure what happened to them...I asked them, 'Please tell me what was it that happened to you?' They can't even remember anything happening to them."

Paul Crouch replied, "What happened to them?"

"Paul, when I felt this atmosphere on me, and I spoke of a word, *FIRE*, like that [Hinn screams "fire"], they were thrown in the air, began to roll real rapidly, and they went into the, what do you call that, like when a baby—a fetal position, with their bodies vibrating from head to toes violently, almost to the place you thought something physically was wrong with them."[253]

Anytime weird, metaphysical shenanigans occur at Hinn's crusades, he makes a spiritual threat to any who obey the Lord's command to "test the spirits" and discern error.

Hinn once warned that those who criticize him will drop dead. "The church was born with power," he said, "going out with greater power. The Bible declares that even those who opposed them dropped dead...Those who touched the anointing were judged instantly...We are about to enter into that dimension. It's going to be a most frightening time for the world, a most glorious time for you. Look, I am telling you what the Lord is telling me."[254]

During this stretch of time that these manifestations prevailed, Hinn's persona took on a very ghoulish voice and appearance. You could literally see the change overtake him, much in the same way you might see a spirit medium be taken over by an evil spirit. One observer noted, "Hinn is now so far gone in his 'ministry' that he is growling and snarling like a beast, and cursing those who resist him. He is also manifesting classic signs of possession, for his voice changes to that of another person at times during his meetings."[255]

At Hinn's Denver crusade in September of 1999, Hinn's voice took on a devilish tone, and he growled in a hideous voice as if in pain. He said through clenched teeth, "If I don't release it, I'll blow up. If I don't release the anointing I'll blow up. I got to release it on somebody." Then he stopped as if he could hear a voice, with his hand cupping his ear, he said, "Yes, lord. I'll do it. I place a curse on every man and woman that will stretch his hand against this anointing. I curse that man who dares to speak a word against this ministry."[256]

While Hinn was seeing this angry anointing in his meetings, John Arnott's *River Revival* was turning into an international phenomenon attracting scores of sign-seekers flying in from every corner of the planet.

Charisma magazine's publisher Stephen Strang interviewed Benny Hinn during Toronto's heyday, and asked him where he thought the latest "revival" was leading. "Well, I can tell you; it's like a river," Hinn responded. "The minute it starts moving, it goes into dry places. I mean the Bible says that God will bring rivers in the wilderness."[257]

Hinn, in his attempt to defend "The River" manifestations seen in Toronto and in his own crusades, actually hit on the key to its source—dry places.

Jesus defined what dwells in "dry places": "When an unclean spirit goes out of a man, he goes through dry places, seeking rest, and finds none. Then he says, 'I will return to my house from which I came.' And when he comes, he finds it empty, swept, and put in order. Then he goes and takes with him seven other spirits more wicked than himself, and they enter and dwell there; and the last state of that man is worse than the first. So shall it also be with this wicked generation" (Matt. 12:43–45).

It would seem that Hinn gave away the secret source of power that fueled the Toronto "revival" and his own simultaneous "fire" anointing. Both ministries fizzled out and for the past several years both had been somewhat quiet. But this was the calm before the storm. When the evil spirit returned from the dry places he brought seven more evil ones along with him and re-emerged in Lakeland in 2008 igniting the wild fires of Todd Bentley who kicked cancer victims in the stomach and boasted of kicking old ladies in the face with his biker boot as a sign of his anointing.

The so-called river movement that began with the holy laughter phenomenon from South African crusader Rodney Howard-Browne, and branched off into the Vineyard churches wrecked many lives.[258] The new wine that the church seemed to be inebriated with included barking like dogs, roaring like lions, clucking like chickens, and what amounted to the animalization of Christianity.[259] Even the secular media took notice and all the major networks visited the Toronto Airport Christian Fellowship and caught people on camera acting mad and blaming it on the Holy Spirit for the whole world to see. It has long been discredited but not before causing much damage to the reputation of the Holy Spirit. Footage from TACF resembled scenes from the old movie *The Snake Pit* that displayed people being given over to their madness in an insane asylum.

One river movement critic rightly pointed out, "Some people try to justify this by saying, 'We know this phenomena we have from Toronto is of God because we asked Him for a fish. He won't give us a serpent' (Matt. 7:11). If you ask for a fish and you get a serpent, you can be sure the serpent didn't come from the Father. If you're holding a snake in your hand, it doesn't look like a mackerel, does it?"[260]

HINN'S ENDORSEMENTS

As already noted, Oral Roberts considers Hinn's ministry an equivalent to a modern-day Noah's ark and, along with Mark Chironna, points to Hinn's ministry as the fulfillment of the coming of Elijah before the return of Christ. All the false prophets looked to Hinn as the top banana until the Elijah List incorporated their assembly of "prophets" and took to the airwaves and Internet television. Even Rodney Howard-Browne, the originator of the holy laughter/drunkenness craze that invaded Toronto and the world, points to Benny Hinn as his source of inspiration and acknowledges Hinn's metaphysical power.

Howard-Browne explained this to Hinn once on Hinn's daily TV program. "I sat down in your chair [upon visiting Hinn's set] and I was pretending to be you. I looked at the camera and picked up one of the video tapes and held it in my hand and I said, 'People, I tell you there's a wonderful anointing!'"

"You were trying to imitate me?" asked a surprised Hinn.

The laughing evangelist replied, "Some people think I'm crazy when I say this, but this is a fact. I was there when it happened! If you've ever seen a movie where somebody got struck by lightening…Well, through the chair, the power of God just come up and hit me…my eyes got big. They [Kent Maddoux and his wife] all felt the presence of God and I just slowly put the video down…For about eighteen hours, I felt that…and right after that the miracle anointing increased in my life. It was amazing!…And even though I was playing, I mean I wasn't doing it mocking, but the anointing of God just came and God touched me. And it's scriptural because the Bible talks about when they took the dead man and threw him on the grave and he landed on the prophet's bones, the person came back to life."

Hinn's warning to the Kentucky conference attendees to leave the service if he ever tells them that he knows the name of angels in glory or that he can visit Jesus in heaven is astonishing considering his claim to paranormal activity.[261] Perhaps he was being careful with his words. Had he warned them to leave the service if he ever claimed that Jesus was going to show up physically in his meetings, they would have to leave. If he told them to ignore any claims that angels show up in his bedroom out of a heavenly portal, they would have to walk out on him.

Hinn's wife Suzanne has been active in a women's group called the Endtime Handmaidens that chases after every false move of a spirit there is. Mrs. Hinn introduced her husband to the late Ruth Heflin, the undiscerning woman infamous for introducing Silvania, the Brazilian gold lady, to the church. Silvania made the circuit of charismatic churches manifesting supposed gold dust all over her face and hair. The dust was later examined and discovered to be nothing but cheap plastic glitter. But even after the evidence was shown, Heflin and Suzanne Hinn continued to insist it was from God. Mysteriously Benny Hinn himself produced the gold dust manifestation on his own face, whether it was the result of a false spirit or a fiendish prank one cannot be sure.

"You know a prophetess sent me a word through my wife," Hinn told a captivated audience during a TBN Praise-a-thon in April of the year 2000. "She said, 'Tell your husband that Jesus is going to physically appear in his meetings.'" (Heflin died of cancer the following September at the age of sixty.)

Hinn then excitedly said to Paul Crouch, "I know deep in my soul something supernatural is going to happen in Nairobi, Kenya. I feel that I may very well come back—and you and Jan are coming too—we may very well come back with footage of Jesus on the platform!" He claimed that Jesus had already been showing up in various places. "You know that the Lord appeared in Romania recently," said Hinn. "And there's a video of it…Paul, do you remember when I came on TBN years ago and showed you a clip of the Lord appearing in our church in Orlando, on the balcony on the wall?…This manifestation of the Lord's face on the balcony, that stayed for eight weeks. Eight solid weeks!…I am prophesying this! Jesus Christ, the Son of God, is about to appear physically in some churches, and some meetings, and to many of his people, for one reason—to tell you He is about to show up! To wake up! Jesus is coming, saints!"[262]

When the Kenya meeting came and went and nothing resembling Jesus showed up in the crowd of a million people, Hinn did not back down, but for a while kept looking for such a thing to manifest.

He also made a wild claim that Jesus was appearing physically to the Arab world. "Now something else is happening that is to me awesome. Absolutely awesome! The Lord is physically appearing in the Muslim world. I'm telling you, Paul, I am hearing it now more and more and more."[263]

Hinn defended his anticipation of a physical visit from Jesus by saying it is biblical since after His death Jesus appeared to many. But what he forgets is the word of the angel who upon Jesus' ascension into heaven said, "Men of Galilee, why do you stand gazing up into heaven? This same Jesus, who was taken up from you into heaven, will so come in like manner as you saw Him go into heaven" (Acts 1:11).

In like manner is not showing up in a crowd somewhere, but when He returns—every eye shall see Him. That's not to say that Jesus has never appeared to anyone in a vision as He did to the apostles Paul and John after His ascension. But these were not physical visits in this earthly dimension as Hinn is anticipating and as many false prophets have claimed to have experienced.

Author Dave Hunt warned, "Now if the real Jesus is going to catch us up and we're going to meet Him in the air, and you're looking for a Christ who, when you meet him your feet are planted on planet earth and he has simply arrived to take over this beautiful kingdom you have established, you have been laboring under a horrible delusion and you have been following the antichrist, not the real Christ."[264]

ANGELIC VISITATIONS

Hinn claims access to the angelic realm. Over the years, he has told incredible stories of heavenly and hellish visitations—some while awake and some in his sleep. One particularly frightening story concerned his wife, Suzanne. "Two o'clock in the morning, I wake up and my wife is choking in bed," Hinn told a wide-eyed Paul Crouch on the October 23, 1999 broadcast of TBN's *Praise* program. "The devil was trying to kill her," Hinn continued. "My wife wasn't acting like my wife. I saw my own wife attacked. It was like the last thing I could handle, I think."[265]

On the other hand, Hinn also reports visits by good angels. Paul Crouch agrees and stated as fact, "I can pray, 'God send my angel to go get him…sic 'em!' " Benny responded, "Do you know why Jesus said if you call twelve legions? One for each disciple—eleven and himself. Which means we don't have one angel each, we have six thousand apiece. Based upon that scripture every believer has a legion of angels. Ecclesiastes 5:6 says speaking the wrong words in their presence will bring us destruction. If we speak something wrong in their presence they will harm us…We don't realize sometimes that our words cause them to move whether positive or negative…The Bible says our words provoke them."[266]

What sort of angels can these be if Crouch can sic them on

people as if they were invisible attack dogs? Hinn's legion sounds pretty frightful as well since Hinn has to watch his mouth so they don't murder him. One of the angels Hinn claims to have contact with is the archangel Michael. Here is his absolutely ludicrous account:

> I awakened half-way in the night and I looked and there was a gentleman—big—looked like a man—six feet...maybe more than that, wearing a hood, black, dressed in black. I couldn't see the face. I saw hands coming out of this horrible looking robe...and long fingers with nails and he came at me to choke me and I was so frightened...And I screamed, "Jesus help me!"...This evil angel dressed in black fought real viciously and kept wanting to come near me but he could not. He was held back. [Describing other angel]...He was more glorious than the other one...I saw a very beautiful wide face, magnificent hair, curly...round curls all around, blond, the blondest blond I've ever seen in my life. I saw bluish eyes that looked through me (blinding white clothes)...Suddenly a third angel comes in...And called him by name. I didn't know who he was till I heard his name. I'm telling you, God is my witness. He called him Michael... And that second he said, "You take care of him."[267]

He's right about one thing—God is his witness. Some of Hinn's angelic visitations sound eerily similar to the stories of UFO abductees—the ones they give while under hypnosis. Later in that same broadcast Hinn recounted:

> For a whole year nearly every night I'd see angels in my room...I never saw them in the daytime. I would only see

them when I'd wake up at night. I'd see them standing in
a corner talking. I sometimes see three, four, and a number
of times again [puts his hand on the Bible]. If you have a
problem, it's your problem, but I'm telling you the truth. I
saw what looked like children, looked just like little kids—
frightened me—Never said a word to me…They'd just look
at me…I got the feeling that, "What does God want with
him?" I'm serious…It almost gave me the feeling of I was
being studied…[268]

Hopefully none of these angels put him on a gurney and inserted
any probes into his body. But, not to worry, according to Hinn's
traveling tenor, Steve Brock, Hinn has power over all devils as was
reported in the August 1997 TBN newsletter. It read: "At a recent
crusade, the Lord gave Steve Brock a powerful word: That as Pastor
Benny shares this testimony [of Hinn casting out demons], whenever he comes to a city, the demons over that city will flee, crying,
'The man of God is coming; the man of God is coming!'"[269]

PROPHETIC TRACK RECORD

Benny Hinn cashes in on the superstitions that he has planted into
people's minds by using his place of power to compel people to
donate to his ministry and that of TBN, as has already been documented. Hinn shared his dream that the prophet Elijah handed off
his rod of authority to him and then with that authority commanded
the people to empty their pockets. He warned TBN supporters that
those who held back from giving would not survive the year 2001, as
was supposedly prophesied by *700 Club* founder Pat Robertson. Yet,
when 2001 came and went there were no casualties to report and no
apologies forthcoming.

On New Year's Eve 1989, Hinn proclaimed that the homosexual community of America would be destroyed in the mid-1990s and attributed that bit of information to the Lord.[270] At that same service, Hinn prophesied that an earthquake would destroy much of the East Coast of America in the 1990s and that Fidel Castro would die at the same time.

More than ten years later in the year 2000, Hinn told the Crouches on *Praise* that he was trying to get his crusade into Cuba. Jan Crouch asked him, "Are you going to Cuba?" Hinn responded, "The thing with Cuba…is the door's opened for us, but I will not go till I have in writing on paper that I'm allowed to preach freely…I want it in writing that I'm free to minister freely and when I get that thing in writing, I'll go…And Cuba's gonna open up no matter what, cause God said it would."[271]

Did God say Cuba would open up to Hinn before or after God told him that Castro would die sometime in the 1990s?

Hinn's track record seems to get worse as time passes. Just before America sent troops to Iraq in 2003, Hinn prophesied over the coming invasion. He went on both *Praise the Lord* and TBN's *Behind the Scenes* programs to get his important message out to all. He also sounded the warning on his own television program. Again he heard another audible voice in the dark in the middle of the night. "I awakened hearing, 'rivers of blood, rivers of blood,' almost shouting it in my ears. And I awakened with the words, 'rivers of blood.' So you can tell this is not going to be an easy future for the world."[272]

Later on in the week, Hinn addressed TBN's studio audience on the *Praise* program. "The Lord revealed to me what's coming in the next few days and weeks with this war with Iraq. I will tell you this…Dangerous days are ahead for this world…Satan is ready to unleash horror and terror on this earth as never before…I saw things that frightened me…If I'll share what I saw with you right now, this studio audience would run out of this studio and get on their face before God...The Lord said that only those who pray will escape."[273]

Part of his mystique comes from his own boyish charm alongside charisma and pure animal magnetism. People are attracted to him, even though he wouldn't be considered a hunk like a Brad Pitt. In fact, he's a little guy with funny hair and past the prime of life. Some of what people call "slaying in the spirit" could well be women swooning over him as they would a popular rock star. This author has spoken to several women who have met him face to face, and all bear testimony to an unnatural attraction—even experienced by discerning women who think he's a heretic.

One glance at the faces at a Benny Hinn crusade tells it all. I've been to his crusades and noticed that the eyes of his admirers never remove their gaze from him and they stare at him glassy-eyed with tears rolling down their cheeks. His reception even surprises him at times. Once he commented to Paul Crouch how governments around the world were receiving him as if he were a head of state. Coming off of airplanes in some third-world countries such as New Guinea, Hungary, Ukraine, Liberia, and the Ivory Coast, government officials would greet Hinn to give him an official welcome. In Trinidad he was "shocked to see a big band playing and the army there and the generals...and thousands of people on the street," Hinn said. "And I think, 'My God, who's here, Jesus?'" "Yeah, he was!" responded Crouch.[274]

AN EARLIER TOUCH OF SANITY

Every now and then Hinn gets it right. Perhaps God has given him warnings against the direction Hinn was taking his ministry.

In June of 1987, Hinn preached a message to his congregation about the dangers of false prophets coming into the church. He said, "Today the Lord has made it very clear to me that I am to warn you today of what's coming...And the Bible tells me if I don't tell you, God will require the blood on my hands!"[275] Could he have been unknowingly speaking of himself when he then said, "Many ministers of the Gospel started right—today they are way off. God will judge them for being way off and forget all good, all righteousness done before."

"What's the message out there today?" Hinn asked rhetorically. "It's a message of ego, pride, and selfishness. It's a message of mine, me, I, show me how to get more!...If I hear prosperity one more time I'm gonna throw up. True prosperity has nothing to do with money! True prosperity is contentment with whatsoever state I am."

He continued, "There's too much today being preached that's not Gospel; and I was preaching it myself because I honestly believed that these men whom I respect must be hearing from God. And if they're saying it, well it must be God. To then discover that the scripture states completely the opposite...You are as tired and as sick of money-hungry, greedy hypocrites to where you almost threw up. They come to empty your pockets, promising you mountains of gold...you haven't gotten one mountain yet."

And sadly, Hinn rightly prophesied, "God is sick of it...I fear for these men. Unless they wake up they may find themselves in a pit they'll not get out of." Later Hinn really hit the proverbial nail on the head. "Any preacher that doesn't preach self-denial, the cross, the blood, is a false prophet."[276]

Wow! How soon he forgot his own wisdom. He admitted later that the one who changed his mind and convinced him that the prosperity gospel was true was none other than Oral Roberts. Hinn testified on the *Praise* program on April 3, 1991 that he invited Oral Roberts to be a guest speaker at his church, that Roberts taught Hinn the give-to-get gospel, and that the Lord later confirmed the teaching. Hinn said, "And the Lord came to me and said, 'Do you believe this or not?' I said, 'Yes, Lord.' He said, 'Now start sowing your seed and thanking Me for the harvest.'"[277]

It didn't take long for Hinn to go headlong into that error and become just as money-hungry as the false prophets he had labeled a few years before. One former Hinn supporter was shocked at just how far Hinn got in his quest for the almighty dollar. This man had been a regular donor to Benny Hinn Ministries and received an invitation from Hinn's staff to join him for supper after his local crusade. The donor was excited about the opportunity. He said:

> The day finally came when we were to meet with him. We were taken by security personnel to a private room where we met twenty to thirty others who were there by special arrangement...Hinn came out in his Italian suit, Rolex, gold, etc. And all along, I thought the man wanted to meet us for something special. He did. He wanted a jet airplane...a new "vision" of the Lord. He wanted all of us to put seed money down on it. Most of the people in the room pulled out their checkbooks and started writing immediately. We felt personally embarrassed, and we did not expect to have the "squeeze" put on us...He took each check, read the amounts out loud to all others and let us all get compared to one another...As soon as the money was collected, he had to leave the room.[278]

Ever since Hinn went along with Oral Roberts, the elder seems to have targeted the younger as his own choice of a successor.

In Hinn's recent bout with clarity, his words of warning apply to Elijah List and to his own work as well:

> The greatest danger in this end times is not poverty, it's not sickness, it's not even persecution; it's deception and if anyone here says, "It cannot happen to me. I am immune to deception"…then you're deceived already. Jesus warns of deception to his own people…Signs and wonders do not determine truth…Signs and wonders can be dangerous when people believe a lie, when they dismiss the truth of God's word and believe things they hear just because somebody says I have a healing ministry; I have a ministry of the signs and wonders or the miraculous. The supernatural does not prove or determine truth; it's the other way around.[279]

Can I hear a hearty Amen!?

CHAPTER ELEVEN

ECUMENICAL ALLIES

The true Christian's number one loyalty must be to the Lord who bought them. If we truly love Him we will be offended when someone insults Him or twists His words, or spreads lies about Him. Jesus told His disciples, "Do not think that I came to bring peace on earth. I did not come to bring peace but a sword" (Matt. 10:34). He then went on to explain that loving Him would mean having to divide from those that don't. Truth divides.

Our loyalty to Jesus gets tested in many ways, but no way more than in our personal associations. Jesus said, "I have come to set a man against his father, a daughter against her mother, and a daughter-in-law against her mother-in-law…He who loves father or mother more than Me is not worthy of Me" (Matt. 10:35, 37).

Most Christians have seen this play out in their own private lives after coming to believe in Jesus and then suffering ridicule and scorn from unbelieving family and friends. It is the cost of discipleship. Yet most Christians are unable to see the same tests of their loyalty to Jesus on the big scale—in their own church life.

One criticism leveled at Christianity by unbelievers is that there are so many different denominations and movements. Yet true believers are united in spirit no matter what their denominational affiliation may be. However, there are many groups that name the name of Christ who are bankrupt of the truth. Discerning Christians must avoid such groups. The apostle Paul taught us how to view this situation. "For there must also be factions among you, that those who are approved may be recognized among you" (1 Cor. 11:19).

Today it is popular to find the lowest common denominator for Christian unity. If a person claims to be a Christian and yet since professing faith in Jesus their lives remain unchanged, how can their testimonies be believed? There are so many who say, "Yeah, I believe in Jesus; I'm a Christian," and yet they still live with their significant other without being married or still carry on getting drunk and taking drugs. There is no noticeable change in their conscience, yet they may attend their seeker-friendly church on Sundays for a quick pick-me-up. The apostle Paul warned us not to associate "with anyone named a brother, who is sexually immoral, or covetous, or an idolater, or a reviler, or a drunkard, or an extortioner—not even to eat with such a person" (1 Cor. 5:11).

He also rebuked the Corinthians for putting up with false teaching and false teachers. "For if he who comes preaches another Jesus whom we have not preached, or if you receive a different spirit which you have not received, or a different gospel which you have not accepted—you may well put up with it!" (2 Cor. 11:4).

We have already seen that TBN's teaching of the prosperity gospel is a different gospel that we should not tolerate. And we see that the great apostasy in the church will have as one of its traits a great love of money as is shown in Christ's letter to the Church of the Laodiceans in the book of Revelation. But there is an even bigger danger lurking on the Christian airwaves—the cry for unity between truth and error and the war cry against all who oppose.

Since the early days of Christian television networks, ecumenical union of Catholics and Protestants has been promoted. However, the same grace has not been extended to non-Catholics by EWTN, the largest Catholic TV network. Catholics have programs on TBN, but no Protestant has their own show on EWTN. Paul Crouch has said that ecumenism was his contribution to the undoing of the Reformation. He often says, "I'm not protesting anything!" in reference to the Protestant Reformation. At the same time he claims to be a direct descendant of Zwingli, one of the Reformers.

But was the Reformation simply one big misunderstanding? Certainly not! The issues that motivated Martin Luther to nail the Ninety-five Theses to the door of the Wittenberg cathedral are still present within Catholicism. All true lovers of Christ Jesus have a biblical mandate to separate from such. And as stated above, love of Jesus is the biggest motivating factor in standing against the modern-day trend of ecumenism. Truth divides professing Christians, as does error.

"There are two kinds of division," wrote Bible teacher Jacob Prasch. "The Bible says there will be factions among you to prove what is true. Ecumenism, of course, is a unity not of God's Spirit; a false unity. The Holy Spirit is the Spirit of Truth. You cannot build the unity of the Spirit on error. To unite with churches that teach salvation comes through 'sacraments,' instead of by being born again, and that practice transubstantiation and praying to the dead, is flagrantly immoral. That is not the unity of the Spirit. Bible believing Christians cannot unite with the false religious system of this world."[280]

And yet the Bible prophesies that this is indeed what will happen in the end times. There will be a one-world religion headed up by the "false prophet" that the Bible refers to as "Mystery Babylon"—a mystery religion that counterfeits Christian unity but is spiritually unfaithful to the Bridegroom and is therefore labeled "The Great Whore." Throughout scripture the Lord uses the symbolism of the adulterous wife to paint a picture of His own chosen people's unfaithfulness to Him.[281]

The Lord said also to me in the days of Josiah the king: "Have you seen what backsliding Israel has done? She has gone up on every high mountain and under every green tree, and there played the harlot." (Jer. 3:6)

The entire book of Hebrews is a warning against the church making the same mistake as the Israelites did in the Old Testament. And the apostle John who penned the book of Revelation warned the church about the very thing that ensnared the Israelites. He ended his first epistle with this warning: "Little children, keep yourselves from idols. Amen" (1 John 5:21). That would make absolutely no sense to the church if idols were merely images that people worshipped in the form of false gods. This was never a temptation to those who name the name of Christ.

However, the Roman Catholic Church is a false system of salvation through sacraments and has idolatry as the core element in its worship. And it's not just the erection of statues representing Jesus, Mary, and the saints that is at the center of the idolatry, though they do play a part. The object of the Roman Catholic adoration is a round piece of bread in the shape of a host, called "the eucharist." Many Catholic churches have set up round-the-clock eucharistic adoration, in which Catholics take turns kneeling before the tabernacles on Catholic altars around the world worshipping a wafer.

Catholic apologist Peter Kreeft, in his 1996 bestseller, *Ecumenical Jihad*, said, "The power that will reunite the church and win the world is Eucharistic adoration."[282] Kreeft lets the cat out of the bag that the round host is the Roman Catholic god. "We see Christ as Eucharist, Christ in the Eucharist; but we see Christ in the Eucharist. We worship the Eucharist because it is Christ."[283]

Charles Spurgeon commented on Catholic idolatry in a sermon titled "A Jealous God." He said, "With what indignation must the Lord look down upon that apostate harlot, called the Romish Church, when, in all her sanctuaries there are pictures and images, relics and statues, and poor beguiled beings are even taught to bow before a piece of bread…I have seen thousands adore the wafer, hundreds bow before the image of the Virgin, scores at prayer before a crucifix, and companies of men and women adoring a rotten bone or a rusty nail, because said to be a relic of a saint."[284]

When the host is taken out from behind the veil of the golden tabernacle, and is put out on display, it is placed in what is called a *monstrance*, a gold host-holder in the shape of a sunburst. This is often used for processions in which the "faithful" can pray to it as it passes by. This is very much a Babylonian practice as many Bible scholars have documented from history. Catholics are taught that Jesus is personally present in these hosts after receiving the priestly blessing and that He is embodied in the round, flat, bread with His entire "body, blood, soul, and divinity." This host then becomes the Catholic's focus of devotion and the means of receiving Christ via the tongue and through the belly and then out the normal course.

The fact that the Catholic god is in the shape of a host is no real mystery when you consider the historical backsliding of Israel when they followed after the Babylonian mystery religions and erected temples to the gods of the constellations. Even though God is called "The Lord of Hosts" throughout the Old Testament, it doesn't mean that He Himself is a host. The "hosts of heaven" is a term used allegorically to describe the saints and angels in heaven of whom He is the Lord. But the literal sense of the "hosts of heaven" is the heavenly hosts—the stars and planets. Though God created them, He forbade His people from worshipping them.

In the book *Graven Bread*, author Timothy Kauffman rightly pointed out that "The eucharist has long held an exalted position in the liturgy of the Catholic Church. In fact, just participating in the sacrifice of the mass is, in and of itself, a form of worshipping the eucharist. Pope John Paul II confirmed this understanding."[285]

And the Catholic faithful traditionally only receive the host and not the wine. If they were being true to their own claim that they are following New Testament teaching on communion, then they would not hold back the cup from the laymen. The Catholic hierarchy justifies this obvious breach with scripture with the twisted logic that all of Jesus is contained in the flat wafer itself. "The Church of Rome states that the bread not only becomes the body of Jesus, but that it becomes His blood as well," wrote Kauffman. "That being the case, it is considered proper to receive the Sacrament of Communion under only one of the two species, i.e., in the form of bread alone. It is held by the Catholic Church that receiving communion under the form of bread alone is sufficient as a fulfillment of Jesus' command. But that is not what the Bible says. That is not what Jesus taught us, and it is not how He asked to be remembered."[286]

How can Bible-believing Christians be expected to embrace the Catholic faith when it so clearly practices idolatry? One Hebrew expert put it well when he said, "Graven images are idols. The Hebrew word for 'worship' is the same word to genuflect, to prostrate, to bow down. When you see a Roman Catholic bowing down to a statue, that is idolatry. Roman Catholic churches are temples of idols. They believe that the bread and wine is transubstantiated, that it's Jesus Christ incarnate. They worship the bread and wine. It's not a memorial to them, it's him. They worship it, then they eat it. This is eating food sacrificed to idols. It's idolatry, it's cannibalism. Those who eat at Jezebel's table! What agreement has the temple of God with idols?"[287]

Spurgeon recognized the implication as well. "Let us above all never have any complicity with this communion of devils, this gathering together of the sons of Belial; and since our God is a jealous God, let us not provoke Him by any affinity, gentleness, fellowship, or unity with this Mother of Harlots and Abominations of the earth."[288]

These are harsh words, indeed. However, today many Evangelical Christians confuse speaking the truth with being unloving. It is not unloving to warn strongly against false doctrines when ignoring them can lead to spiritual darkness that is growing in the church.

CHARISMATIC RENEWAL

TBN from its inception has hosted Catholic priests and laymen and aired Catholic programming. TBN's website has links to many Catholic leaders such as Fr. Rick Thomas, universalist priest Fr. Michael Manning, and Catholic inner-healer Francis MacNutt—all who are considered "charismatic Catholics."

One of the main unifying ingredients of the sort of Catholic-Pentecostal ecumenism TBN promotes is the claim of spirit baptism with the evidence of speaking in other tongues, which are not really languages (which is the meaning of "tongues" in scripture) but babbling in gibberish.

Pentecostal denominations began to spring up early in the twentieth century. It is debatable how much of the movement was a result of a true outpouring of God the Holy Spirit and how much was founded upon counterfeiting the real. It was probably a mixture of the two. It is so much a part of the sinful condition of man to want to imitate the spiritual gifts he sees in others so as not to feel left out.

For instance, the Jesus movement among the hippies in the 1960s and 1970s was, I believe, a true outpouring of God. Longhaired and barefoot, young people flowed into the makeshift tent of Calvary Chapel in Costa Mesa, California. The traditional organ was replaced with acoustical guitars and contemporary Christian music was born. God also mightily used evangelists like Nicky Cruz, Mario Murillo, and David Wilkerson. Many young people who were rejected by society and would never be welcomed into mainstream churches dressed as they were, flocked to Calvary Chapel's tent meetings with their Bibles in tow. The altar calls packed the front of the tent with young people crying over their lost condition, then weeping for joy of their salvation. While Pastor Chuck preached on the soon return of Jesus, expressions of excitement lit up the faces of these outcasts of society, proving God is no respecter of persons.

At the same time, interest in Bible prophecy and the recognition of the soon return of the Lord was popularized by books like Hal Lindsey's *The Late Great Planet Earth* and Salem Kirban's novel *666*. The zeal and exuberance for the Word of God was electrifying and contagious. Young people were truly on fire for the Lord and spread the excitement wherever they went.

These things were surely a threat to the devil who no doubt thought he had thoroughly conquered the baby-boomers with sex, drugs, and rock 'n roll. The trappings of the world no longer had a hold on these new saints, so the god of this world had to resort to a different strategy if he was to squash this revolt to his sovereignty. He would have to deceive from within, just as he did in ancient church history. This modus operandi did the trick in the days of Emperor Constantine when he helped merge Christianity with paganism creating a hybrid religion, and it would work for him again by blurring the distinctions between the holy and profane.

His target: disenfranchised church leaders from the mainline denominations and the Roman Catholic Church—all of whom were losing their young people by the score to new independent Bible fellowships like Calvary Chapel. The devil and his agents seemed to be working on many different fronts to try and stem the tide of mass evangelism. He even infiltrated the Jesus movement with men of the spiritual nature of "Simon the magician" in the book of Acts, who came up with formulas to operate "spiritual" gifts, discouraging the baby Christians from waiting upon the moving of the Holy Spirit for the true gifts. By doing so, the Holy Spirit was quenched from the lives of those who were deceived into thinking the gifts of the Holy Spirit could be learned by one's own efforts.

The mainline denominations came up with their own answer to the Jesus movement and called it the "charismatic renewal." Renewal leaders such as Episcopalian priest Dennis Bennett and inner-healers John and Paula Sandford gave workshops at major conferences that taught people how to initiate spiritual gifts themselves and then claim the Holy Spirit as the source. National conferences on the Holy Spirit sprang up heartily embracing Roman Catholics who learned how to counterfeit the "gifts of the spirit" from them.

Roman Catholic historian John Vennari documented the early days of the Catholic Charismatic Renewal in an article published in the Catholic Family News entitled "A 'Catholic' Charismatic Extravaganza." He was referring to a conference sponsored by the Franciscan University at Steubenville celebrating the thirtieth anniversary of the Catholic Charismatic Renewal "in Pittsburgh 'where it all began.'" Vennari attended the conference on June 27, 1997 as an observer, not a participant.[289] He noted that the conference drew out seventy-five hundred Catholic participants with the theme "Under the Spout where the Glory Comes Out." It took place at David Lawrence Convention Center whose stage was decorated with "a large crucifix, a Divine Mercy poster, and an image of Our Lady of Guadalupe."

Vennari reported that the first speaker at the thirty-year anniversary conference was Kevin Ranaghan who "recounted that in the early days, in order to 'grow in the spirit,' he and his friend sought spiritual advice from a Protestant prayer group."[290] Vennari identifies Ranaghan as the founder of the movement who, along with his wife Dorothy and their colleagues at Duquesne University, received counsel from an Episcopalian minister involved in the charismatic renewal "in search of a greater influence of God in their lives." They then joined up with Catholic lay leaders Ralph Martin and Steve Clarke who introduced them to the book, *The Cross and the Switchblade*, the story of former gang leader Nicky Cruz as told by Pentecostal preacher and founder of Teen Challenge, David Wilkerson. As they read about the transformed lives in the book "they sought to receive a similar experience," reports Vennari. Ranaghan also recalled the role of the Full-Gospel Businessmen's Association in the birthing of the Catholic Charismatic Renewal.

One of the participants at the thirty-year anniversary celebration testified that he received the baptism of the Holy Spirit when they broke up into several groups for prayer at the conference. "I asked to be prayed with for the baptism of the Holy Spirit," Vennari quotes the man as saying. "They simply asked me to make an act of faith for the power of the Spirit to work in me. I prayed in tongues rather quickly."

The false teaching that a person can pray in another tongue simply by an act of faith was popularized by the late "Father" Dennis Bennett, an Episcopalian canon that Paul Crouch refers to as "a pioneer of Pentecost." He most likely was the Episcopalian minister referred to by Kevin Ranaghan.

"The 'Reverend' Kevin Martin of Episcopal Renewal Ministries said that Dennis Bennett '...was directly responsible for the charismatic movement in the Roman [Catholic] Church that now reaches into the millions.'"[291]

Bennett wrote the best-selling books *Nine O'Clock in the Morn-*

ing and *The Holy Spirit and You*, and is said to have led over twenty-five thousand people into the "Release of the Holy Spirit."[292] On a visit to TBN's *Praise the Lord* on September 24, 1991, one month before his death, Bennett told the TBN audience how to "release the spirit." "Just begin to offer him sounds like a child. Just praise him and don't do it in English." As he gave this instruction he began making little sounds, muttering in a way to lead people to imitate him. "Let him out! Release Him!" Bennett cajoled the TV audience. "We need to release him! We got to let him out!"[293]

After Bennett's interview ended on that night's *Praise* program, Paul Crouch introduced his next guest, TV preacher Casey Treat. "Now Casey Treat is coming to teach us how to channel this for the kingdom of God," Crouch announced.

Crouch's guest informed the viewers that they needed to be yeast in the church to spread this concept throughout the body of Christ. Treat explained that we Christians need to activate what's already inside of us. "We have the controls in our hands really," Treat thundered in excitement. "The ball's in our court. God's done his part and now we have to activate it!"

"It simply proves the point from another angle," added Paul Crouch, "that it is up to us, isn't it?"[294]

These men just stole the work of the Holy Spirit right out of the lives of many gullible viewers. Unfortunately, this false teaching that Christians need to learn how to tap into the power of the Holy Spirit as if God has no say in the matter has been at the core of the working of counterfeit gifts. And while Dennis Bennett and others like him were spreading this error among the mainline denominations and the Catholic Church, the late John Wimber, the powerhouse behind the Vineyard churches, was popularizing these ideas within the Evangelical community as a whole with the help of Fuller Seminary and TBN.

PROTESTANT PUBLIC RELATIONS

By the time Christian television became a reality in the 1970s, the "charismatic [ecumenical] renewal" had overshadowed the Jesus movement and taken center stage. The differences between the two movements by then was totally blurred and the new "Christian" broadcasters such as Pat Robertson, Jim and Tammy Bakker, and of course Paul and Jan Crouch confused things even further by creating networks that embraced the good and the bad and presented both as a united faith.

All of these major Christian broadcasters broke down the dividing walls between Catholics and Protestants, ignoring five hundred years of differences as if they never existed. The Crouches in particular used a system of propaganda to promote the false idea that the Roman Catholic Church was just one of many Christian denominations. Paul Crouch has simplified and repeated his call for Christian unity under the banner of brotherly love, belittling of doctrine, and ridiculing of those he terms "heresy hunters," so much that it has permeated the collective Christian consciousness of many professing believers. Crouch's favorite sayings are heard repeated by so many people because of the tone of ecumenical correctness he has established. If any Christian journalist writes anything critical of a TV preacher—Protestant or Catholic—he or she is immediately called a "heresy hunter" by well-meaning but pre-programmed TBN viewers. This group-think mentality has become a real spirit of error in the body of Christ today.

Ecumenism with Catholicism has always been fashionable in the charismatic church. Pioneers in Christian television like Oral Roberts and Kathryn Kuhlman prided themselves on including Roman Catholics in their gatherings. The most famous evangelist in the world, Billy Graham, embraced Catholic participation in his crusades very early on, even sharing the platform with Catholic priests. He also received an honorary doctorate in 1967 from a Roman Catholic College and told his audience that the "Gospel that founded this college is the same Gospel which I preach today."[295]

And Graham received the International Franciscan Award in Minneapolis in 1972 by the Franciscan friars for his work in ecumenism.[296]

Christian television celebrity Rex Humbard followed the same ecumenical code set by Roberts and Kuhlman and praised the Catholic pope. He wrote in his March 1980 newsletter about his visit with the late John Paul II, "As we talked together, I sensed more and more that our mission is the same: to build the body of Christ; to uplift our brethren in the Lord; to win the world for the kingdom; to share that shining message that Jesus gave us to share...'You are loved.' I wish you could have been there, standing by my side, as I shared those few moments with Pope John Paul II. For those were milestone moments in my own personal life, in my spiritual life."[297]

What is this earthly kingdom all the televangelists want to build without the King? Since the Catholic Church teaches that the pope is the "Vicar of Christ," he would be the ultimate head of any earthly unity between Catholics and Protestants. The pope would be at the top of the heap, not C. Peter Wagner. Author Dave Hunt describes the meaning of "Vicar of Christ": "Vicarious Christi [in] Latin, [is] the English translation Vicar of Christ. Well, vicarious is the Latin equivalent, interestingly enough, of the Greek, anti. So, Vicarious Christi, literally, I guess a literal translation would be antichrist."[298]

Christian author and researcher Roger Oakland has been sounding the alarm for years of the Roman Catholic Church's New Evangelization program, which will require all Christians to worship the "Eucharistic Christ," acknowledging the host to be the actual body, blood, soul and divinity of Christ. A refusal to acknowledge this false teaching is what led many true Christians to be burned at the stake during the Inquistions at the time of the Reformation. In his commentary called, "Will Every Knee Bow?" Oakland writes:

> How do Protestant Charismatics perceive the "New Evangelization" program that will require embracing the Eucharistic Christ? Will they accept this Roman Catholic "Jesus" or reject? What if down the road, signs and wonders begin to happen? What if manifestations of the Eucharistic Jesus are associated with healings and the casting out of demons? What if these miracles and appearances were so convincing, people of other faiths were drawn to an experience-based "Christianity" which eventually causes them to bow to the Eucharist?[299]

It would seem that the televangelists, rather than warning Christians about the dangers of the ecumenical movement, are at the forefront in selling out the truth for the sake of a perceived unity. That's not to say that there are no true Christians in the Roman Catholic Church, for I believe there are, but that the official teachings of Rome are at odds with biblical faith. Not all professing Catholics even understand the doctrines of their own church that nullify salvation by grace through faith. When all true believers from all traditions are taken up in the rapture, those who are left will have no restrictions in unifying the harlot church. The ground for that is already being laid.

Kuhlman's biographer, Jamie Buckingham, wrote an editorial for the charismatic magazine, *Charisma*, back in March 1992, called "Bridge Builders." In it he praised all the ecumenical efforts of both Pentecostals and Roman Catholics by name. "At the 1977 Kansas City ecumenical-charismatic conference he warned: 'We cannot have unity based on doctrine. Doctrine will always separate the body of Christ.'"[300]

But the apostle Paul warned Timothy over and over again to pay heed to his doctrine. "Take heed to yourself and to the doctrine. Continue in them, for in doing this you will save both yourself and those who hear you" (1 Tim. 4:16). It then goes without saying that by allowing false doctrine in the church we cannot save ourselves or our hearers.

During one of Paul Crouch's ecumenical diatribes he brushed off the Catholic doctrine of the eucharist as unimportant. "Some of these even so-called doctrinal differences...are simply matters of semantics," he said on *Praise the Lord*. "One of these things that has divided us [referring to transubstantiation] all of these years shouldn't have...we were really meaning the same thing but just saying it a little differently...So I say to the critics and theological nitpickers, 'Be gone, in Jesus' name!' Let's come together [with Rome] in the spirit of love and unity."[301]

On another *Praise the Lord* program, Crouch's guest was Benny Hinn who told the story of a time when he joined a Catholic nun for communion in the chapel of a convent. She knelt down and began to pray and Hinn, reluctant at first, joined her only to find that the anointing he was so familiar with was present in the room. Hinn said that God told him that it's a matter of faith, not doctrine. God supposedly said, "'To her I'm in the elements, to you I'm in the room, but to me I'm still here.' In other words, according to your faith be it done unto you...You know what I think? I don't think He cares!"[302]

"He's in both!" Crouch agreed. "But see, the heretic hunters get in there and we argue over the doctrine of transubstantiation and all over this garbage...the letter kills."[303]

And yet Crouch would brand his own ancestor Zwingli a heretic hunter since he defended the biblical teaching that the Lord's Supper was memorial in nature. In fact, during the Inquisition, the nature of the eucharist "was at the very center of it. It is a historical fact that the worship of the eucharist was once considered the indication of a true Christian, and that refusal to bow before the eucharist was considered the mark of a heretic. Such heretics were at the mercy of the Tribunals of the Inquisition."[304] And we all know that many true believers were tortured and burned for denying transubstantiation.

However, sometimes the truth slips out, even out of the mouths of ecumenists like Benny Hinn. During a *Praise the Lord* program on May 7, 2002 Hinn said that the current pedophile priest scandal rocking the Catholic Church was an open door to preach the Gospel to millions, implying that Catholics aren't true Christians.

Yet he is the same man who told Paul Crouch on live TV that whenever he wants an audience with the pope, Hinn can arrange it for him. One picture of Paul Crouch meeting with the last pope is proudly hanging in the hall of TBN's headquarters in Costa Mesa, California, along with another picture of Jan Crouch greeting the late Mother Teresa. These send a clear message to all visitors that the Crouches recognize the Roman Catholic Church as just one of many valid expressions of Christianity. What they won't tell you is that the Roman Catholic Church's official position is that non-Catholic denominations are a lesser expression of Christianity and that only the Mother Church is the true church.

Benny Hinn revealed one reason for wooing Catholics when he was the key speaker at the "West Coast Conference on the Holy Spirit" that was held in 1991 at Melodyland, a charismatic church in Anaheim, California. "I've never seen more Holy Ghost Catholic powerful precious people than I'm seeing here tonight," Hinn said, flattering his Catholic audience. "When the Catholics get the Holy Ghost, they become powerful." Then he followed with the financial appeal. "And you right here…get your envelopes out…get your checkbooks out, all you precious Catholics and Pentecostals and charismatics…get your checkbook out!"[305]

When TBN launched its new affiliate television station in Rome in 1994, the newsletter making the announcement also displayed the same picture of Crouch shaking hands with the pope. That same newsletter boasted of Crouch's longstanding relationship with the Catholic Church. "Praise the Lord! Pope John Paul II can now see, not only many of the TBN programs, but also, some of the special Catholic programs and guests that appear quite often…Plus great programs with Fr. Rich Thomas, Fr. Ralph DeOrio, who has a great healing ministry, as well as our regular program, *Alive* hosted by Fr. Michael Manning. Jan will want to show her heart's desire meeting with Mother Teresa and let's not forget a new series with Fr. Ricardo Castellanos, our wonderful Spirit-filled brother in Miami who moves and operates in the precious gifts of the Spirit! Wow! The body of Christ IS coming TOGETHER as we all move closer to Jesus!"[306]

When the pope visited Denver, Colorado in 1993 for World Youth Day, Matthew and Laurie Crouch hosted the television coverage. Matt Crouch told the TBN audience, "One of the greatest events happening right here in Denver, Colorado is his holiness, Pope John Paul II right behind us here…What we're doing here is a big festival that has been sponsored by the Vatican…and actually TBN was a co-sponsor of this event."[307]

It is disturbing to hear non-Catholics refer to the pope as "his holiness," but it has become commonplace on Christian television. Paul and Jan Crouch refer to him that way, as do Jack and Rexella Van Impe on their prophecy program seen on TBN, *Jack Van Impe Presents.* By doing so, they are acknowledging the pope's supremacy as the leader of the Christian world, a bad trend from the view of those who hold the Bible as the final authority in the church.

REVIVAL OF CATHOLIC MYSTICISM

Since the popularity of the Emergent church and cross-pollinating writers such as Catholics Henri Nouwen and Brennan Manning, Evangelicals have begun to adopt monastic practices such as contemplative prayer. Their books have popularized the idea of "Christian" mysticism, which is just a nice way of saying they teach occult practices. All of a sudden, it's considered cool to sit in the lotus position in front of a lit candle and incense and make one's mind a blank, expecting to contact the god within.

The apostolic/prophetic movement has picked up the craze but renamed the mindless meditations. They call it "soaking" and even teach classes on the subject. John Arnott, at Toronto Airport Christian Fellowship charges big bucks to learn these newly named monastic practices. The Bible would call these "influences from the East"—something we are to stay away from. "For You have abandoned Your people, the house of Jacob, because they are filled with influences from the east and they are soothsayers like the Philistines" (Isaiah 2:6; NASB).

By practicing such occult methods that Catholic monks shamelessly admit they got from Zen Buddhism, Christians are unknowingly opening themselves up to the same demonic activities that were common in the Dark Ages.

It is a well-known fact that the newly canonized saint Padre Pio, well-known for his stigmata, would be thrown into his lit fireplace by whatever evil spirits were toying with him. Even Pio admitted that he didn't know if his bloody hands, feet, and side were from God or his annoying poltergeist.[308]

In the new prophetic wave of the charismatic church there are many testimonies of metaphysical madness happening that used to only happen in Catholic monastic circles. Manifestations such as levitation, bilocation, stigmata, and insanity are now commonplace.

An Associated Press story on Oral Roberts years ago quoted him as saying, "The devil came to my room just a few nights ago, and I felt those hands on my throat and he was choking the life out of me." He called for his wife who came in and cast it out.

TBN "prophet" Mark Chironna testified during the Spring 2001 Praise-a-thon, "I went through severe paranoia. Literally I was paranoid and a principality visited my room every night at three in the morning. There were two red eyes in a dark cape. And I did what Wigglesworth did; and I did what Lester Sumrall did and it didn't work...six months later it broke, a bright light was at the foot of the bed and it was an angel of the Lord. And I was not allowed to turn the light on, but I followed the light. It went down into the living room floor and God said, 'When you step there you'll be stepping into greatness.'"[309]

One of the Elijah List's prophetesses who is a frequent guest on Christian television made a call for charismatics to embrace charismatic Catholics. She encouraged Christians to embrace Catholic mysticism. She wrote, "I believe the Lord wants to up-cap the ancient wells of the Catholic mystics and desert fathers and bring them into the Protestant Church."[310]

The late Faith teacher Kenneth Hagin testified that he witnessed a floating lady at a prayer meeting once. (Sounds like a horror movie to me.) After praying for the lady to be healed he said, "The power of God was there! It was that power which lifted her up. Now if she had responded to that—if she would have believed it and accepted it—it would have healed her...What was that power that lifted her up out of the chair? What was that power that pulled her away from it so that she was sitting in front of it, suspended in the air? It was dynamic Holy Ghost power!"[311]

Sounds like dynamic demonic power to me—she wasn't even healed or helped in any way. They should have called in an exorcist.

Some of the more famous Catholic mystics manifested some pretty scary metaphysical traits. EWTN ran an episode of *Super Saints*, hosted by Bob and Penny Lord that focuses on their saints and featured what they call "the flying saint," and they weren't referring to Sally Field. He is St. Joseph of Cupertino who is said to have levitated every time he looked at a crucifix. His fellow monks had to tie a tether to his ankle so he wouldn't float off into space.

St. Theresa of Avila is reported to have levitated and made mysterious noises down in her throat—not unlike some similar manifestations that can be observed at a prophetic signs and wonders gathering. St. Catherine of Siena used to levitate herself off the floor several times a day and speak in unknown tongues according to Hugh Farrell, a former Catholic priest.

Now even stigmata is showing up in charismatic circles where signs and wonders are the focus. Besides bragging about glory gold dust and "toking the holy ghost," prophetic prankster John Crowder wrote in his blog of what he calls the "blood sign." He shared about a lady named Lucy Rael who used to work in the ministry of T. L. Osborne and received the stigmata. Not only did she excrete blood from her hands, but holy oil flowed as well. He said those in his ministry "tenderly refer to it as 'stiggy!'"[312]

FINAL DESTINATION

This mystical trend borrowed from Catholic mystics and contemplative monks have become a point of power for the Catholic Church over her Protestant children.

The winds of ecumenism are blowing stronger and stronger and are leading to the ultimate unification of Catholics and Protestants. Could this be why the adulterous church of the last days before the return of Jesus is referred to as the Mother of Harlots? Who is she the Mother of? This spiritual harlot—untrue to the Bridegroom—has rebelled against His Word and rejoins with her estranged offspring, the younger harlots, so she can again be Mother Church?

The writing is on the wall!

CONCLUSION

Television is a powerful medium. Success on the small screen can be a snare for any human being. When strangers run up to a televangelist to touch the hem of their garment, the attention can go to anyone's head. Yet it can be a powerful voice for the spreading of the Gospel of Jesus Christ. Many seeds of the Word of God have been sown into the hearts of many viewers who channel-surf and run across a meeting like the *Harvest Crusade* or stumble upon the man-on-the-street evangelism of *The Way of the Master*.

Anything God uses for good can be corrupted for evil. Only the Day of Judgment will tell how many people were actually saved due to hearing the Gospel on television verses how many people rejected Jesus Christ because of how He was represented on the very same airwaves.

In these perilous times before the return of Jesus Christ, Christian satellite networks and television stations consistently misrepresent the Lord, fleece His sheep, and live lavishly on the widow's mite. The spirit of antichrist already dominates the airwaves that have supposedly been dedicated to the Lord Jesus Christ.

For those of us who anticipate the rapture of the saints before the time of the seven-year tribulation when the wrath of God is poured out upon an unbelieving world, we have not placed our hope in this world. We see all things coming together as was prophesied thousands of years ago. When the rapture happens, Christian television will still be on screens around the world. There will not be any interruption in scheduling.

Many, many people who call themselves Christians will be left behind, in denial, refusing to believe that they missed the shout, "Come up hither!" They will find some other explanation and they will be happy to finally be successful in joining with other "Christians" to form the visible one-world church. They will think they have achieved the purpose of Jesus' prayer to the Father that we would all be one.

They will have dynamic leaders who will continue to hold up the kingdom of this world as the prize to be gained. They will accumulate riches and hold hands with one another singing "We are the World" until all hell breaks loose and what they have amassed goes up in flames.

We are already seeing the beginning of the formation of the harlot church as God seems to be giving people over to their delusions. It seems to make no sense that so many people can be deceived by such obvious spiritual chicanery on the television airwaves. But if they do not test what they're being taught, then they have not a love for the truth. We were warned ahead of time:

> The coming of the lawless one is according to the working of Satan, with all power, signs, and lying wonders, and with all unrighteous deception among those who perish, because they did not receive the love of the truth, that they might be saved. And for this reason God will send them strong delu-

sion, that they should believe the lie, that they all may be condemned who did not believe the truth but had pleasure in unrighteousness. (2 Thes. 2:9–12)

This is a call to the flock of God to wake up and wise up and return to the Word of God. Test all things by its teachings. If something doesn't sound right, don't go along with it. Remember the Lord's warning:

Behold, I am coming quickly! Hold fast what you have, that no one may take your crown. (Revelation 3:11)

And John the Revelator's words:

Little children, keep yourself from idols. Amen. (1 John 5:21)

FOR FURTHER INFORMATION SEE
http://www.apostasyalert.org

ENDNOTES

Chapter 1—Trailblazing Televangelists

1. Catechism of the Catholic Church, ©1992, Libreria Editrice Vaticana, Citta Vaticano, pg. 102, para. 460
2. T. L Osborn, *You are God's Best: Special TBN Edition*, ©1984, Osborn Ministries, Tulsa, OK, p. 31
3. Anne Gimenez, Rock Church broadcast, Daystar Network, circa 2000, tape on file in author's collection
4. Evelyn Roberts, guest on son's Richard Roberts TV show, "Something Good Tonight, The Hour Of Healing," Sky Angel, circa 2001, tape on file
5. Patti Roberts, *Ashes to Gold*, ©1983, Word Books, Waco, Texas, pg. 170
6. B.D. Hyman, daughter of Hollywood actress Bette Davis, Sky Angel, circa 1999, tape on file
7. Kenneth Copeland interviewed by Pat Robertson, *700 Club*, May 4, 2000, tape on file
8. Paul Crouch, *Praise the Lord*, TBN, circa 1989, tape on file
9. Steve Munsey, Sky Angel telethon, circa 1999, tape on file
10. Richard Roberts, ORU broadcast, Sky Angel, circa 2000 tape on file

11. Oral Roberts, *Miracle of Seed Faith*, ©1970, Fleming H. Revell Co, Tulsa, OK, p. 51

12. *Ibid.* p. 19

13. *Ibid.* p. 24

14. Matthew 6:24

15. Oral Roberts being interviewed by Paul Crouch Sr. and Paul Crouch Jr., Behind the Scenes, TBN, October 15, 2008

16. Oral Roberts, *The Call*, ©1971, Avon Books, New York, p. 158

17. Mike Murdock, *Inspiration Today*, Inspiration Network, November 8, 2008

18. Ellen Parsley, *Celebration*, Daystar TV Network, Dallas, March 6, 2000, tape on file

19. Walter Martin, "Miracles" quoting philosopher David Hume, audio tape on file

20. Roberts, *Ashes to Gold*, p. 119

21. *Ibid.* p. 120

22. *Ibid.* p. 121

23. David Edwin Harrell Jr., *All Things are Possible: The Healing and Charismatic Revivals in Modern America*, ©1975, Indiana University Press, p. 6

24. Roberts Liardon, *God's Generals* video series, tapes on file

25. Jamie Buckingham, *Daughter of Destiny*, ©1976, Bridge Publishing, South Plainfield, NJ, p. 219

26. *Ibid.*, p. 221

27. *Ibid.*, p. 229

28. *Ibid.*, p. 221

29. *Ibid.*, p. 220

30. Oral Roberts, interviewed by Paul Crouch Sr. and Paul Crouch Jr., *Behind the Scenes*, TBN, October 15, 2008, viewed in the online archives at www.tbn.org

31. Oral Roberts, interviewed by Paul Crouch Sr. and Paul Crouch Jr., *Behind the Scenes*, TBN October 22, 2008, viewed in the online archives at www.tbn.org

32. R. W. Schambach, *Praise-a-Thon*, TBN, April, 2000, tape on file

33. Harrell, p. 156

34. William Nolen, *"In Search of a Miracle,"* McCall's Magazine, 9/74, quoted in Jan, 2005 *Berean Call*

35. Buckingham, *Daughter of Destiny*, pp. 251-252

36. Roberts, *Ashes to Gold*, pp. 109-110

37. Dru Axtell, *I Thought it was God*, ©1988, New Leaf Press, Green Forest, AR, pp. 106-107

38. *Ibid.*, p. 154

39. Buckingham, *Daughter of Destiny*, p. 250

40. Roberts, *Ashes to Gold*, pp. 82-83

41. Roberts, *The Call*, p. 157

42. Buckingham, *Daughter of Destiny*, p. 271

43. Axtell, *I Thought it was God*, pp. 127, 152

Chapter 2—The End Times at TBN

44. For a good study of bible Prophecy, see J. Dwight Pentecost's *Things to Come; A Study in Biblical Eschatology*, ©1958 Dunham Publishing - republished by Zondervan, Grand Rapids

45. See Abraham's argument with God in the 18th chapter of Genesis where God said He would not destroy Sodom if He could find ten righteous men therein.

46. TBN Web Site, www.tbn.org as of 10/2008

47. Paul Crouch, *Praise-a-Thon*, TBN, Fall 1999, tape on file

48. *Ibid.*

49. Jan Crouch, *Macedonian Call Praise-a-Thon*, TBN, 7/22/91, tape on file

50. June 2000 TBN Newsletter

51. Benny Hinn, interviewed by Paul and Jan Crouch, *Praise the Lord*, TBN, 10/23/99, tape on file

Chapter 3—The Great Apostasy

52. TBN Newsletter Vol. XIV No 1—January 1987 pg. 2, emphasis in original

53. TBN Newsletter Vol. XVII, No. 1—January 1990, pg. 2, emphasis in original

54. R. W. Schambach, *Praise-a-Thon*, TBN, Fall 1990, tape on file

55. Benny Hinn interviewed by Paul Crouch, *Praise-a-Thon*, TBN, 11/9/90, tape on file

56. Paul Crouch, *Praise-a-Thon*, TBN, Spring 1992, tape on file

57. Phil Munsey, *Cornerstone Network Telethon*, 10/1/99, tape on file

58. TBN newsletter Vol. XVII, No. 3, March 1990, p. 1, emphasis in original

59. Matthew Crouch, *"The Omega Code Set for Fall Release,"* *Charisma Magazine*, August 1999, pp. 16-17

60. Kim Clement interviewed by Matthew Crouch, *Praise the Lord*, TBN, 6/1/99, tape on file

61. Rev. 3:10

Chapter 4—Aquarian Conspiracy Revisited

62. Marilyn Ferguson, *The Aquarian Conspiracy*, ©1980, J. P. Tarcher, Inc., Los Angeles, distributed by St. Martin's Press, New York. pg. 27

63. *Ibid.*, pg. 28

64. Phil Munsey, *Praise the Lord,* TBN, 10/10/97 presented in Paw Creek Ministries' video tape, "*Trinity Broadcast Network: Temple to the Gods and Goddesses*" available at: http://pawcreek.org/

65. *Ibid.*

66. *Ibid.*

67. Walter Martin, audio tape, "*Schismatic Sheep,*" pt. 1, circa 1986, audio tape on file

68. Kim Clement, *Praise the Lord,* TBN, 2/6/2000, tape on file

69. Jim W. Goll, "*Paradigm Shifts for the 21st Century,*" Northwest Revival News, www.nrn.net

70. Quoted from a Toronto Airport Vineyard audio tape, dated 4/10/94

71. Logos2, blogger on the Zola Board, www.zolalevitt.org

72. Marcia Montenegro, *The Secret: Chicken Bones for the Hungry Soul,* M.C.O.I Journal, p. 15

73. *Path of Discovery,* ©1987, United Church of Religious Science, Los Angeles

74. *Ibid.,* p. 21

75. Stan Monteith, Radio Liberty radio program, 8/30/07

76. Johanna Michaelsen being interviewed by host Dr. Stan Monteith, Radio Liberty radio program, 8/30/07

77. Kim Clement, *Call Me Crazy, But I'm Hearing God,* ©2007, Destiny Image Publishers, Shippensburg, PA, p. 149

78. *Ibid.,* p. 61

79. *Ibid.,* p. 203

80. Advertisement on Todd Bentley's Web site, www.freshfire.ca

81. Manly P. Hall, *The Initiates of the Flame,* ©1922, Publisher Unknown, p. 57

82. *Ibid.,* p. 83

Chapter 5—Redefining Church

83. John Ankerberg and John Weldon, "*The Facts on the New Age Movement,*"©1988, Harvest House Publishers, Eugene, Oregon, pg 23

84. John Eckhardt, *The Apostolic Church*, ©1996, Crusaders Ministries, p. 14

85. Rick Joyner, *Morning Star Prophetic Bulletin*, May 1996, pp. 1-2

86. *Ibid.* p. 3

87. Glenna Jehl, *Revival in Baltimore*, 1/21/98, http://revival. godchasers.net/0002.html, p. 2

88. *Ibid.*

89. Kim Clement, http://www.kimclement.com/itin/history/ history.htm

90. Tommy and Jeannie Tenney, *Vision of the GodChasers. Network*, http://www.godchasers.net/vision.html

91. Tommy Tenney, "*The God Chasers*"©1998, Destiny Publishers, Shippensburg, PA, pg. 7

92. 1Ki 13:3b-5

93. Tenney, *God Chasers,* pg. 36

94. Matthew Fox, Creation Spirituality web site, http://www. creationspirituality.com/about-cs.shtml

95. Kim Clement, http://www.kimclement.com/itin/history/ history.htm

96. Kim Clement, *Praise the Lord*, TBN, 7/8/2000, tape on file

97. Kim Clement, *Praise the Lord*, TBN, 6/1/99, tape on file

98. Paul Crouch, *Praise the Lord*, TBN, 8/12/93, tape on file

99. Matthew Crouch, *Praise the Lord*, TBN, 3/21/2000, tape on file

100. Matthew Crouch, *Behind the Scenes*, TBN, 8/30/2000, tape on file

101. Matthew Crouch, *Praise the Lord*, TBN, 1/18/2001, tape on file

102. Paul Crouch, *Behind the Scenes*, TBN, 8/30/2000, tape on file

103. Kim Clement, http://www.kimclement.com/warriors/fall99/warriors2.htm

104. Kim Clement, http://www.kimclement.com/warriors/summer2000/kims_personal_journal.htm

105. Kim Clement, *Praise the Lord*, TBN, 7/7/97, tape on file

106. *Ibid.*

107. Jacob Prasch, – *"Vain Philosophies of the World—Study in Colossians 1,"* audio tape #PRA-1148, available at www.moriel.org

108. Kim Clement, *Praise-the-Lord*, TBN, January 18, 2001, tape on file

109. Kim Clement, *Praise-the-Lord*, TBN, 3/23/01, tape on file

110. Kim Clement, *Praise-the-Lord*, TBN, 6/1/99, tape on file

111. Tommy Tenney, *God Chasers*, Introduction

112. Matthew Crouch, *Praise the Lord*, TBN, 7/8/2000, tape on file

113. *The Donning Int'l Encyclopedic Psychic Dictionary*—www.bible.ca/tongues-dictionary-occult-donning.html.

114. Curtis Crenshaw, *"Christian Fortune-Tellers Never Get It Right, Either"* quoted on PFO's Web page at www.pfo.org

115. Tenney, *God Chasers*, pg 81

116. Kim Clement, *Praise-the-Lord*, TBN, 1/18/2001, tape on file

117. Kim Clement, *Praise-the-Lord*, TBN, 3/21/2000, tape on file

118. Kim Clement, *Praise-the-Lord*, TBN, 2/6/2000, tape on file

119. Kim Clement, *Praise-the-Lord*, TBN, 3/23/01, tape on file

120. Tenney, *God Chasers,* p. 97

121. *Ibid,* pg. 26

122. Kim Clement, *Praise-the-Lord,* TBN, 6/1/99, tape on file

123. Scott Bartchy, quoted in Los Angeles Times, December 27, 2003, *"Spiritual Blend Appeals to People of Many Faiths"* by K. Connie Kang, Times Staff Writer, on-line edition: http://www.latimes.com

124. Kim Clement, *Praise-the-Lord,* TBN, 7/7/97, tape on file

125. Bill Hamon interviewed by Gary Greenwald, *Saints Arise,* Sky Angel, circa 2001, tape on file

126. Richard Fisher, *"Christian Fortune-Tellers Never Get It Right, –Either"* PFO's Web page at www.pfo.org

127. Tommy Tenney, *Praise-the-Lord,* TBN, 1/18/2001, tape on file

128. *Ibid.*

129. Bill Hamon interviewed by Gary Greenwald, *Saints Arise,* Sky Angel, circa 2001, tape on file

130. Tenney, *God Chasers,* pg. 2

131. Kim Clement, *Praise-the-Lord,* TBN, 3/21/2000, tape on file

132. Walter Martin, *"Psychic Phenomena,"* streaming audio heard at www.waltermartin.org

133. Fisher, *"Christian Fortune Tellers,"* www.pfo.org

134. Gary Gilley, *The Calvary Contender,* Vol. XVII, No. 22, Nov. 15, 2000

Chapter 6—The Root of All Evil

135. greed. Dictionary.com. *The American Heritage® Dictionary of the English Language, Fourth Edition.* Houghton Mifflin Company, 2004. http://dictionary.reference.com/browse/greed

136. Paul Crouch, *Praise-a-Thon*, TBN, 4/10/1992, tape on file

137. Lu 3:14

138. 1Ti 6:8

139. Php 4:11

140. See Rev. 18:22-23

141. Paul Crouch, *Praise-a-Thon*, TBN, 4/10/1992, tape on file

142. *Ibid.*

143. *"A New Way of Giving,"* Time, July 24, 2000, www.time. com/time/magazine/article/0,9171,997528,00.html

144. Ole Anthony, quoted in *"As Seen on TV,"* by Abe Opincar, *San Diego Reader*, July 29, 1993

145. Paul Crouch, *Praise-a-Thon*, TBN, 4/1/1991, tape on file

146. David Wilkerson, cover letter enclosed with his pulpit series, Dec. 2000

147. See Jackie Alnor, "Jezebel and the Frog Prince," http://www. apostasyalert.org/REFLECTIONS/jezebel.htm

148. Juanita Bynum, *Praise-a-Thon*, TBN, 11/07/2003 tape on file

149. Paula White, *1999 Charisma Women's Conference*, Sky Angel, 5/29/99, tape on file

150. John Avanzini, *Praise-a-Thon*, TBN, 4/10/1992, tape on file

151. Paul Crouch, *Praise-a-Thon*, TBN, 11/4/91, tape on file

152. Paul Crouch, *Praise-a-Thon*, TBN, 4/1/91, tape on file

153. Though Avanzini's program was canceled, Paul Crouch still endorses him and cites his false teachings favorably.

154. John Avanzini, *"Principles of Biblical Economics,"* TBN, circa 1999, tape on file

155. *Ibid.*

156. *Ibid.*

157. *Ibid.*

158. Paul Crouch, *Praise-a-Thon*, TBN, 11/7/95, tape on file

159. Jan Crouch, , *Praise-a-Thon*, TBN, 7/22/91, tape on file

160. Larry Thomas, *The Inkhorn,* Vol. 5, No. 1, February, 1994

161. John Avanzini, *Praise-a-Thon*, TBN, circa 1999, tape on file

162. Walter Martin, *"Little Gods in the Church,"* audio tape on file

163. Avanzini has since been replaced on the *Praise-a-Thons* by Mark Chironna who teaches the same "give to get" message.

164. http://en.wikipedia.org/wiki/Morris_Cerullo

165. Jackie Alnor, *"Morris Cerullo's 'Miracle Explosion' in Philadelphia,"* The Christian Sentinel, 1992, http://www.cultlink.com/sentinel/morris.html

166. John Avanzini, *Praise-a-Thon*, TBN, Fall 1990, tape on file

167. John Avanzini, *Praise-a-Thon*, TBN, 4/1/91, tape on file

168. John Avanzini, *Praise-a-Thon*, TBN, 11/7/90, tape on file

169. *Ibid.*

170. John Avanzini, *Praise-a-Thon*, TBN, 11/6/90, tape on file

171. Greg Laurie, CSN radio network broadcast, circa 2000

Chapter 7—Spiritual Extortion

172. R.W. Schambach, *Praise-A-Thon*, TBN, Fall 1990, tape on file

173. Paul Crouch, *Praise-a-Thon*, TBN, 4/5/2001, tape on file

174. Frederick K. C. Price, excerpted from his book, *Faith, Foolishness, or Presumption?*

175. Paul Crouch, *Behind the Scenes*, TBN, 4/14/00, tape on file

176. R.W. Schambach, *Praise-A-Thon*, TBN, Fall 1999, tape on file

177. R.W. Schambach, *Praise-A-Thon*, TBN, Fall 1999, tape on file

178. R.W. Schambach, *Praise-A-Thon*, TBN, 4/2/01, tape on file

179. R.W. Schambach, *Praise-a-Thon*, TBN, 4/1/91, tape on file

180. Jacob Prasch, *"Be Consoled,"* Tape #PRA-1008, available at www.moriel.org

181. Jan Crouch, 1994 vintage *Highlights of TBN* program, tape on file

182. Paul Crouch, *Praise-a-Thon*, TBN, April 1999, tape on file

183. Paul Crouch, *Praise-a-Thon*, TBN, 4/4/01, tape on file

184. Martin Lloyd-Jones, *"The Glory of God,"* circa 1960, http://mlj.org.uk/frames.htm

185. Benny Hinn, 1989 New Year's Eve message, audio tape on file

186. Benny Hinn, *Praise-a-Thon*, TBN, Spring 1999, tape on file

187. *Ibid.*

188. R. W. Schambach, TBN Newsletter February, 1998, Vol. XXV, Number II

189. Paul Crouch, TBN Newsletter March 1999, Vol. XXVI, Number III

190. See the fourth chapter of Matthew

191. R. W. Schambach, *Praise-a-Thon,* TBN, Fall 1999, tape on file

192. Jacob Prasch, *"Faithful and Unfaithful Bride"* audio tape on file

193. Benny Hinn, message at Orlando Christian Center, June 21, 1987, transcript by Bud Press

194. *Ibid.*

195. *Ibid.*

196. *Ibid.*

197. Benny Hinn, *Praise-a-Thon*, TBN, 4/3/91, tape on file

198. *Ibid.*

Chapter 8—Lifestyles of the Rich & Famous

199. David Edwin Harrell, Jr., *"All Things Are Possible,"* ©1975, Indiana University Press, Bloomington, p. 74

200. Jacob Prasch, *"People's Opinions or God's,"* a study of II Sam. 5 & 6, audio tape #PRA1129 available at www.moriel.org

201. Charles Capps, *"Seed-Faith Book Turns Life Around,"* Oral Roberts' magazine, *Abundant Life*, May/June 1987, pg. 5

202. Jamie Buckingham, *"Something Good Has Happened,"* Oral Roberts' magazine, *Abundant Life*, May/June 1987, pg. 7

203. 1998 On-line forum, Thread: *"TBN is insane":* alt.fan. bob-larson

204. Apodaca, Patricia, "Southland Ranks as TV's Bible Belt," Los Angeles Times, Orange County edition, 1/12/98

205. Video is available from Paw Creek Ministries, 5110 Tuckaseegee Rd., Charlotte, NC 28208, www.pawcreek.org

206. Joseph Chambers, *"Temple to the Gods & Goddesses,"* Paw Creek Ministries, tape on file

207. Paul Crouch, *Praise-a-Thon*, TBN, Spring, 1999, tape on file

208. From the *TBN 1994 highlights* program, tape on file

209. *Ibid.*

210. Dorothy Coslet, Letter to the Editor column, *Charisma*, Sept 1998, pg. 10

211. J. Lee Grady, *"Jan will be Jan,"* Charisma, June 1998, pg. 48

212. Jay Leno, *The Tonight Show*, 12/26/96

213. TBN brochure, *"Fall 1997 Programming Highlights"*

214. Kelly Whitmore, interview 6/6/2001

215. *Behind the Scenes*, 12/28/2000, tape on file

216. Paul Crouch, *Praise-a-Thon*, TBN, 4/4/2001, tape on file

217. Paul F. Crouch, Jr. open letter to *Charisma Magazine* dated November 12, 2007

Chapter 9—Proliferation of False Prophets

218. Dr. Hugh J Schonfield, *The Passover Plot*, ©1965, Random House Inc., New York, cover jacket

219. See 2 Cor. 4:4 that identifies Satan as the "god of this age."

220. Manifest sons/Latter Rain doctrine refers to two interlinked movements from the 20th century. Apologetics Index defines them this way: "The teaching that in the last days, a 'new breed' of Christians will arise—the "Manifest Sons of God"—who will have super-natural spiritual power and be instrumental in subduing the earth."—"Heretical movement popularized by Franklin Hall, William Branham, George Warnock, John Robert Stevens, etcetera. Elements of Latter Rain teachings are today being taught within certain renewal and revival movements." See: www. apologeticsindex.org

221. Eph 1:22 - "And hath put all things under his feet, and gave him to be the head over all things to the church..."

222. Earl Paulk, *Praise the Lord*, TBN, circa February 2000, Tape on file

223. Paul Crouch, *Praise the Lord Newsletter*, Vol. XIV, No. X, October 1987, pg. 1

224. *Ibid.*, pg. 2

225. Rick Joyner, *MorningStar* program, aired 2/14/2000 on SkyAngel, tape in file

226. Deut. 4:2; Deut. 12:32; Prov. 30:6; Rev. 22:18.

227. Ernie Gruen, "Documentation of the Aberrant Practices and Teachings of Kansas City Fellowship" (Grace Ministries,) pp. 223, 227. Can be read online at: http://www.intotruth. org/kcp/Abberent%20Practises.pdf

228. John Wimber, *Equipping the Saints* magazine, Vol. 3, No. 4/Fall 1989, *"Introducing Prophetic Ministry,"* pg. 30

229. John Wimber, *Praise the Lord*, TBN, January 25, 1994, tape on file

230. Wesley Campbell, date unk., tape on file

231. Stacey Campbell, date unknown, tape on file

232. Jacob Prasch, *"The Proliferation of False Prophets"* video interview by author in 2001

233. Mike Bickle, Fall 1989 Grace City Report, *"The Necessity of Judging Prophets,"* pg. 20

234. Teri Lee Earl, *"Trouble in Prophet Land,"* online at www. harvestnet.org

235. Paul Crouch, *Praise the Lord,* TBN, March 3, 1994, tape on file

236. Paul Cain, quoted in Ernie Gruen's "Documentation," pg. 218

237. Lester Sumrall, a clip from Roberts Liardon's video series, *"God's Generals,"* tape on file

238. Al Dager, quoted in *O Timothy* magazine, Vol. 7, Issue 3, 1990

239. Walter Martin, audio tape *"Schismatic Sheep"*—pt. 2, tape on file

240. Dave Hunt, *"Word-Faith Movement"* message spoken © Calvary Chapel Lehigh Valley on 2/28/99

241. Per Oral Roberts at the *ICBM Conference* 6/20/2000, tape on file

242. Matthew Crouch, *Behind-the-Scenes,* TBN, 10/18/02, tape on file.

243. Chironna hosted Hamon on TBN on November 17, 2003 where he credited Hamon as his own teacher in moving in the prophetic.

244. Bill Hamon, interviewed by Gary Greenwald, *"Saints Arise"* program, Sky Angel, August 30, 1999, tape on file

245. See video, *"The Great Apostasy: The Lost Sign,"* produced by the Christian Sentinel, this author's own production, for taped documentation of both Bennett and Howard-Browne

explaining this false teaching. Tape available at www.moriel. org

Chapter 10—The Forerunner Ministry

246. Benny Hinn, *"Freedom from Deception Revival,"* November 2008 Benny Hinn Crusade, Kentucky International Convention Center, Louisville, KY, seen on YouTube
247. *Ibid.*
248. Author Unknown, "New Wine", *The Forerunner Ministry*, www.grmi.org/renewal/new-wine/articles/history/14.html
249. Hinn, *Freedom*, Nov. 2008
250. Benny Hinn, *Praise the Lord*, TBN, 11/9/90, tape on file
251. Benny Hinn, *Praise the Lord*, TBN, September 13, 1999 (transcript by Mike Oppenheimer)
252. Benny Hinn, *Praise the Lord*, TBN, Fall 1999, tape on file
253. Benny Hinn, *Praise the Lord*, TBN, October 23, 1999 (transcript by Mike Oppenheimer)
254. Benny Hinn, *Praise the Lord*, TBN, circa 2/2000, tape on file
255. Tricia Tillin, Banner Ministries, *"Benny Hinn and his Anointing: Report on the Denver Crusade,"* online report at: http://www.banner.org.uk
256. Benny Hinn, Denver 1999 footage played on *Praise the Lord*, TBN, September 13, 1999, tape on file
257. Benny Hinn, *Charisma Magazine* television program on TBN, 4/25/95
258. For more information on The River/Toronto see books, "Weighed and Found Wanting," by Bill Randles, and "When New Wine Makes a Man Divine," by Roger Oakland.
259. *"The Animalization of Christianity"* was the topic this author spoke on at the *1995 EMNR Conference* in Atlanta

260. Jacob Prasch, Audio series *"Gifts of the Spirit - Part 1,"* PRA1022, tape on file

261. Hinn, *Freedom,* Nov. 2008

262. Benny Hinn, Spring 2000 Praise-a-Thon, TBN, video on file

263. *Ibid.*

264. Dave Hunt, Audio Tape #DH11, *The Seduction of Christianity,* undated tape on file

265. Benny Hinn, *Praise the Lord,* TBN, 10/23/99, tape on file

266. Benny Hinn, *Praise the Lord,* TBN, 7/23/2000, tape on file

267. *Ibid.*

268. *Ibid.*

269. TBN newsletter, August 1997, Vol. XXIV, No. VIII

270. Benny Hinn at OCC on 12/31/89, per *"God's Superman,"* compilation of transcripts by researcher Bud Press

271. Benny Hinn, *Praise the Lord,* TBN 1/9/2000, tape on file

272. Benny Hinn, *Praise the Lord,* TBN, 12/23/02, tape on file

273. Benny Hinn, *Praise the Lord,* 12/29/02, t on file

274. Benny Hinn and Paul Crouch, *Praise the Lord,* 5/12/99, video on file

275. Benny Hinn, audio from OCC sermon, June 21, 1987, transcribed by Bud Press

276. *Ibid.*

277. Benny Hinn,, *Praise the Lord,* TBN, 4/3/91, tape on file

278. Testimony of "D. H.", dated 10/15/2000, emailed to author

279. Hinn, *Freedom,* November 2008

Chapter 11—Ecumenical Allies
280. Jacob Prasch, *"Curses and Christians,"* Moriel Newsletter, June 1998, p. 1

281. See the book of Hosea

282. Peter Kreeft, *Ecumenical Jihad,* ©1996, Ignatius Press, San Francisco, p. 164

283. *Ibid.,* p. 162

284. Charles Spurgeon, *"A Jealous God,"* quoted at Bible Bulletin Board at www.biblebb.com

285. Timothy Kauffman, *"Graven Bread,"* ©1994, White Horse Publications, Huntsville, AL, p. 55

286. *Ibid.* pp. 107-108

287. Jacob Prasch, study in Second Corinthians, audio tape on file

288. Spurgeon, op. cit.

289. John Vennari quoted from an undated article copied from Catholic Family News and distributed by Richard Freeman

290. *Ibid.*

291. Rev. Ed Hird, *"Anglican Pioneer in Renewal,"* Anglican Renewal Ministries of Canada website: http://www3. bc.sympatico.ca/st_simons/arm12.htm

292. *Ibid.*

293. Dennis Bennett, *Praise the Lord,* TBN, 9/24/91, tape on file

294. Paul Crouch, *Praise the Lord,* TBN, 9/24/91, tape on file. See Christian Sentinel video, *"The Great Apostasy: the Lost Sign,"* for clips from this telecast.

295. *Smokescreens,* ©1983, Chick Publications, Ontario, CA, p. 56

296. *Ibid.* p. 57

297. *Ibid.,* p. 41

298. Dave Hunt, *"What Does Antichrist Mean?"* http://www. thebereancall.org/node/1855

299. Roger Oakland, *"Will Every Knee Bow?"* http://www. understandthetimes.org/commentary/c27.shtml

300. 1998 news release from Way of Life Literature's Fundamental Baptist Information Service

301. Paul Crouch, *Praise the Lord*, TBN, 10/17/89, quoted in *"A Woman Rides the Beast,"* by Dave Hunt, p. 405

302. Benny Hinn, *Praise the Lord*, TBN, 2/11/92, tape on file

303. Paul Crouch, op. cit.

304. Timothy Kauffman, *"Graven Bread,"* p. 54

305. Benny Hinn, TBN broadcast of the *"West Coast Conference on the Holy Spirit,"* 4/12/91

306. TBN newsletter, Vol. XXI, No. IX, September 1994, *"Rome—On The Air!"* p. 1

307. Matthew Crouch, *Behind the Scenes,* TBN, 8/13/93, clip of World Youth Day events, tape on file

308. EWTN tape on Padre Pio, on file

309. Mark Chironna, *Praise-a-Thon,* TBN, April 2, 2001 tape on file

310. www.keepersofhisgates.com/catholicmystics.htm

311. Hagin, Kenneth E., Faith and Power: Two Ingredients for Receiving Healing, part 1, pg. 8

312. John Crowder, Sons of Thunder blog, 7/9/08 http://sonsofthunderpublications.blogspot.com